*Dedicated to the prisoners of the Japanese
who never came home*

NEVER SURRENDER

NEVER SURRENDER

Dramatic Escapes from Japanese Prison Camps

Mark Felton

Pen & Sword
MILITARY

First published in Great Britain in 2013 by
Pen & Sword Military
an imprint of
Pen & Sword Books Ltd
47 Church Street
Barnsley
South Yorkshire
S70 2AS

Copyright © Mark Felton, 2013

ISBN: 978-1-78159-022-5

A CIP catalogue record for this book is
available from the British Library.

Typeset in 11/13pt Palatino by
Concept, Huddersfield, West Yorkshire

Printed and bound in England by
MPG Printgroup

Pen & Sword Books Ltd incorporates the imprints of Pen & Sword
Aviation, Pen & Sword Family History, Pen & Sword Maritime, Pen &
Sword Military, Pen & Sword Discovery, Wharncliffe Local History,
Wharncliffe True Crime, Wharncliffe Transport, Pen & Sword Select,
Pen & Sword Military Classics, Leo Cooper, The Praetorian Press,
Remember When, Seaforth Publishing and Frontline Publishing.

For a complete list of Pen & Sword titles please contact
PEN & SWORD BOOKS LIMITED
47 Church Street, Barnsley, South Yorkshire, S70 2AS, England
E-mail: enquiries@pen-and-sword.co.uk
Website: www.pen-and-sword.co.uk

Contents

Acknowledgements

A great many thanks to the following individuals and institutions that kindly assisted me during the researching and writing of this book: Jill Durney of the MacMillan-Brown Library, University of Canterbury, New Zealand; Alistair Macdonald; Franklin D. Roosevelt Library & Museum; The Australian War Memorial, Canberra; The Australian National Archives; The National Archives (Public Record Office), London; Ron Taylor of the Far East Prisoners of War Association; US Marine Corps Historical Archives; Brigadier Henry Wilson and the wonderful staff at Pen & Swords Books; and my editor Barnaby Blacker. Finally, many thanks to my amazingly accomplished wife Fang Fang, whose advice and assistance is dearly appreciated.

Introduction

17-year-old Private Bill Young escaped from the Japanese by accident, and although he was caught, his life was probably saved as a result. On 19 February 1943 Young had been slaving away for the Japanese as part of working parties that were constructing an airfield at Sandakan in northeast Borneo. Along with his comrade, 28-year-old Miles Pierce, Young had 'nicked off' during the lunch break to the local village to try and obtain some more food. When the two men returned fifteen minutes later they discovered the airfield in an uproar. 'It came as a bit of a shock, on getting back to the airfield, to see the Nips jumping up and down, and waving their hands about. The air was alive with activity as two hundred gangs of fifty men each stretched on down the mile long, white granite-like strip ... the guards were busy counting, and recounting their charges. Ichy, ne, san, si, go, roco, the cadence came loud and clear,' recalled Young. 'Clear enough for us to realise that we were in the cacky poo.'[1]

Both men had already experienced punishment at Sandakan over minor infractions of camp rules and they had no intention of giving themselves up for a severe beating or worse now that they had been discovered missing from their work party. They could have been accused of attempting to escape and killed. 'It was either return to the fold, or be bold, and stay out in the cold; so escape seemed to be the safest way out,' said Young. 'I always carried a little bit of a map that showed quite clearly that there was only a couple of inches to go across Borneo, right turn, and then, 6 inches past the coffee stain, and we'd be home free in Australia; a piece of cake? A piece of half baked cake.' Both

1

men did not get far before they were recaptured. 'We were dragged over beside the boiler and beaten so badly that, as it was reported to the War Crimes Commission, we'd "both died" ...'[2] The Japanese mercilessly beat and abused Young and Pierce before shipping them off to Kuching to stand trial. They were found guilty of attempting to escape and sent to serve out their sentences at Outram Road Jail in Singapore. If they had not 'accidentally' escaped in 1943 Young and Pierce would have perished along with nearly all of the other prisoners on the Sandakan Death Marches in 1945. Such was the fickle nature of life and death under the Japanese.

During the Second World War the Germans and Italians took prisoner 151,041 British, Australian, Canadian and New Zealand servicemen, as well as 24,400 Indian soldiers. Countless films, television programmes and books have highlighted the brave escape attempts that many of these prisoners made. Stories like *The Wooden Horse*, *Colditz* and *The Great Escape* have all entered the popular imagination. Escape appears in these works to be not only the duty of every able-bodied POW, but also a sport. Colditz Castle was packed full of Allied officers who had made repeated attempts to escape – they were a hard core of plucky and determined men seemingly unbowed by capture. Several hundred Allied POWs successfully escaped from captivity in Germany, Poland and elsewhere and made it to freedom and a chance to fight another day.

In the Far East, the Japanese captured 73,554 British, Australian, Canadian and New Zealand servicemen and women, as well as around 55,000 Indians. Of this number only a tiny handful managed to escape and get home again. Escape is not a word usually associated with Japanese POW camps; instead we read and watch stories about death, suffering and survival, *The Railway Man* being the latest film to deal with those themes.

The reasons why so few Allied prisoners successfully escaped from the clutches of the Japanese are relatively straightforward, and they make those escapes that did succeed all the more remarkable. The first barrier for the Far Eastern POWs was distance. If an Allied POW successfully escaped from a camp in Germany he had several options. He could try to get to Switzerland, Spain or Sweden, all neutral nations where he could be spirited to Britain.

By ship, England was but a few hours sailing time from Occupied Europe. In the Far East the nearest Allied territory was Free China, Australia or India, and most of the Japanese camps were concentrated in Thailand, Malaya, Indonesia, the Philippines, Eastern China, Korea or Japan. They were normally hundreds, and in some cases thousands, of miles from Allied lines. The geography was also fearsome as compared to Europe – trackless jungles, massive mountain ranges, dry plains and huge shark-infested oceans.

The second barrier was the assistance the escapee could expect to receive in Asia. A healthy resistance network operated in France, Belgium and the Netherlands, not to mention in Occupied Scandinavia, all able to assist with a POW's safe passage. As well as local resistance groups and escape lines, the British had in place their own agents from MI9 dedicated to helping prisoners escape from German clutches in Europe. In the Far East, the story was quite different. In many parts of Asia guerrilla groups operated, many of them Communist. Some groups worked for the Allies, some worked for Japanese puppet regimes, and some worked for either side or for themselves. MI9, Special Operations Executive (SOE) and the American OSS all attempted to create networks that could reach into the prison camps, but (with some exceptions) it was chaotic at best and made doubly difficult by the Japanese refusal to report the locations of POW camps to the Red Cross, leaving many hundreds undiscovered until the end of the war.

Another barrier was the treatment of recaptured escapees. In Europe, with the exception of the famous Great Escape from Stalag Luft III where Hitler ordered the execution of fifty British and Allied airmen, a recaptured evader could expect a period of solitary confinement in the camp 'cooler' followed by return to the general prisoner population. Repeat offenders would find themselves sent to 'escape-proof' prisons like the infamous Colditz Castle. Escapers were not subject to torture, starvation or corporal punishment. In the Far East recapture usually meant death. The Japanese treated prisoners according to their own military code, not the Geneva Conventions, so escape was 'desertion' punishable by death by firing squad or public beheading. Others had their death sentences commuted to periods of imprisonment that were so harsh that death often followed later. Not for Allied POWs in the Far East the luxury of considering escape as a 'sport' or even as one's solemn duty – in Asia it was entered into only when all other options for survival had been exhausted. One was permitted only a single opportunity, and most failed.

A fourth point that hindered successful escape by the Far East POW was his ethnicity. Indian POWs had some opportunity of passing themselves off as Tamil rubber estate workers in Malaya or Singapore, but for Caucasian POWs their faces, height, build, skin, and eye and hair colour made them stick out like the proverbial sore thumb the moment they left the camp. And there would usually be little chance of passing themselves off as 'neutral' Europeans because even after a few months in Japanese captivity, a starvation diet, tropical diseases and slave labour had left them suspiciously thin and sickly.

A fifth point was the attitude of the locals to Allied POWs in the Far East. Many Asians, particularly those in Indonesia, despised their colonial masters and would not help whites to remain free. Others, such as the Chinese and Borneans, sympathised with POWs but were often not willing to risk Japanese retribution helping them. The Japanese, like the Nazis, quickly established a climate of fear among the populations that they had conquered. The *Kempeitai* Military Police was given virtually *carte blanche* powers over everyone, and it abused its authority through shocking displays of brutality towards anyone even suspected of harbouring the smallest 'anti-Japanese' sentiments. Hundreds of thousands of men, women and children were put to death by the Japanese during their occupations – shot, beheaded, disemboweled, burned alive or tortured. Most native populations were completely terrorised by their Japanese overlords to the point where very, very few would risk helping their former colonial masters to reach Allied lines. It was often the case that locals handed Allied evaders over to the Japanese in order to collect a cash reward, demonstrate their 'loyalty' to the new regime, or sometimes to enact a personal revenge against their former oppressors, for the Japanese worked hard to foster nationalism and collaboration in the Greater East Asia Co-Prosperity Sphere. In some cases, locals murdered Allied escapers on sight, and there were cases of POWs actually being hunted like wild animals by gangs of armed natives.

Even though escaping from a Japanese POW camp meant almost certain death, staying put was not a much better option. In Europe, Allied POWs escaped so that they could rejoin the war effort, thereby fulfilling their duty. In the Far East many men attempted escape merely in the desperate hope of living. In camp after camp previously fit young men were reduced within the space of a few months to diseased, emaciated skeletons by deliberate Japanese policy. Red Cross parcels were virtually non-existent, and any form of international or neutral oversight forbidden. At any time, a prisoner might be summarily executed for some real or imaginary minor offence. Starved, beaten, exposed to every tropical disease in the book, denied practically all medical treatment, subjected to horrific 'punishments', and forced to labour on dangerous and back-breaking construction and mining projects for their masters, survival became a grim numbers game.

Of the 50,016 British servicemen and women who were captured by the Japanese, 12,433 died in captivity. That is one in four. The Australians fared even worse: 7,412 died out of a total of 21,726. One in three. Of the Indian prisoners, about 11,000 died out of approximately 55,000. One in five. The death rate for Allied prisoners of the Japanese (excluding Chinese) was, according to the Tokyo War Crimes Tribunal, 27.1 per cent or seven times the rate for those taken prisoner by the Germans or Italians. Most of these deaths were the result of deliberate policy, largely created by Tojo, of slavery, torture, starvation, disease and summary execution.

This book details escapes by British, Australian, American, Chinese and Indian prisoners from the Japanese all over Asia. It also tells the stories of some incredible acts of resistance by those who stayed put inside the camps. As you read these stories you will notice that most of those who escaped did not make it to freedom. Some died in the jungle, some were recaptured, tortured, imprisoned or even executed. But even though the odds were so very, very long, a tiny handful of extremely brave, resourceful and lucky men did somehow get back to Allied lines. The men who made it during the war were able to tell their governments exactly how the Japanese were treating POWs, their horrific stories of murder and brutality on an almost unimaginable scale shocking and revolting the politicians and citizens on the home front and acting as an important propaganda tool against the Japanese. So many never made it home, and today the rows upon rows of white headstones in cemeteries from Thailand to Japan, and Manchuria to Java are a visceral reminder of Japan's murderous POW policy and the humanitarian disaster that was unleashed against defeated men.

Chapter 1

Escape is Forbidden

The prisoners, for fairly obvious reasons, always have the feeling of being on the edge of a volcano and we find the mentality of our captors so complex when compared to our own that it is difficult to estimate just what is going to happen.

Captain R.M. Horner, Singapore, 1942

Four young white men stood on an idyllic beach with their backs to the gently lapping sea. In times past the beach had resounded to the sounds of fun and pleasure, but now it had become something sinister and terrible. Close by, a group of senior British and Australian officers stood watching the horrific events that unfolded with dreadful certainty. 'Take aim' barked out a Japanese officer who stood beside the firing party – four turbaned Indian soldiers armed with British Lee-Enfield rifles. The prisoners tensed but bravely faced down their executioners having refused the blindfolds that the Japanese officer had offered them a few moments before. 'Fire!' The rifles crashed out a volley that echoed along the wide and empty Changi Beach in Singapore, startled seabirds lifting off with a cry. Cordite smoke hung in the warm, humid air. The four prisoners were not dead, only wounded. They lay moaning on the sand with their hands tied behind their backs, their blood staining the yellow sand a dark red. Their leader, 39-year-old Acting Corporal Rodney Breavington, called out asking the Japanese to finish them off and end their suffering.

7

The senior officers watching could only shake their heads in disgust and mutter epithets under their breath. A Japanese barked out a series of commands and the Indians fired several more times at the prone men until they were dead. Then the bodies were unceremoniously rolled into the graves that the prisoners had dug for themselves before the execution. Such was the punishment for attempting to escape from the Japanese.

'If the POWs believed they were victims with rights, to the Japanese they were a sullen, disgraced mob, who had lost their rights as individuals and were to be treated as such.'[1] Captain R.M. Horner wrote at the time that the prisoners, for 'fairly obvious reasons, always have the feeling of being on the edge of a volcano and we find the mentality of our captors so complex when compared to our own that it is difficult to estimate just what is going to happen.'[2] In fact, the cultural gulf between the Japanese and their POWs was virtually impossible to bridge and would lead to a great deal of suffering, both intentional and accidental.

Although the Japanese government had signed the Geneva Convention of 1929 it had not been ratified by the *Diet*, the parliament in Tokyo, so therefore Japanese armed forces were not bound by its terms. This fact eliminated at a stroke the legal protections afforded to prisoners of war in other theatres, such as those fighting the Germans and the Italians. Instead, the Japanese governed their POWs according to their own harsh military code. Surrender was a disgraceful and illegal act under Japanese military law, and the Japanese made no allowances for the fact that Allied troops who surrendered came from an entirely different mindset and culture, where the needless sacrifice of lives when military objectives could no longer be achieved was deemed pointless, and an honourable surrender humane. The Japanese described the Geneva Conventions as 'The Coward's Code', and they meant it. The Allied soldiers had lost their status as combatants when they had raised the white flag and were now effectively *persona non grata*. Their lives had only been spared because the God-Emperor Hirohito had deigned to do so, and their lives now belonged to the Emperor to do with as he wished.

Some writers have made much of the fact that the Japanese treated captured German and Austro-Hungarian prisoners exceedingly well during the First World War. This is certainly true, but the reasons why they treated POWs like guests in 1914 and like slaves in 1941 are simple. In 1914 Japan, then an ally of Britain, wanted its place in the sun, its seat at the table of the Great Powers. The Japanese military at this time went out of its way to treat European prisoners well, thereby countering any negative view about a rising non-Anglo-Saxon power having a right to rule over Asian territories. If the behaviour of the Japanese military is examined during the 1894–95 Sino-Japanese War and the 1905 Russo-Japanese War astonishing cases of massacre, cruelty and ill-treatment of prisoners and civilian populations are found. The activities of the Japanese in China in 1931 and 1937 again point to a wholesale disregard of internationally accepted standards of behaviour on and off the battlefield. By the early 1930s the Japanese had broken with Britain and were being propelled down the path of rampant nationalism and reaction against the Western Powers, who were commonly viewed as attempting to frustrate the 'right' of Japan to expand overseas for their own selfish and racist reasons. The experience of prisoners in Japanese hands during the First World War was not atypical of Japanese behaviour in wars both before and after 1914–18. 'We were dealing with a fanatical and temperamental people who, for all practical purposes, only played to the rules when it suited them to do so,' remarked General Percival, who himself had been a prisoner of the Japanese.

On the issue of escape the Japanese military was curiously confused. Escape was every soldier's duty under The Hague and Geneva Conventions, and although the Japanese did not apply the Hague Conventions to their POW policy, this did not remove the duty of Allied soldiers to follow it. The Japanese mocked Allied prisoners for their perceived 'cowardliness' in being captured, yet it would surely follow in Japanese logic that any prisoner who tried to escape was for a brief moment truly a soldier again, and had therefore in some way regained his martial honour. Yet, instead of taking this view, the Japanese generally treated captured escapers with a brutality that was both sadistic and revealed the moral vacuum at the heart of their military machine.

9

In fact, escape was about the worst possible 'crime' that a prisoner could commit in the Japanese military mentality.

Escape was to the Japanese a particularly dangerous transgression because it revealed that their 'slaves' were not subservient enough, not cowed and frightened enough of the all-powerful Imperial Army. Importantly, the prisoners had not accepted their 'shame' – a significant factor in Japan. Many examples were made in order to terrify Allied POWs into becoming better slaves for their masters but, though beaten and humiliated, they never accepted that role, and many of them took it upon themselves to remind their Japanese masters that they would not be cowed and that they felt no shame for their present circumstances. They escaped from camps and work parties, sabotaged forced labour projects, disobeyed orders, argued with Japanese officers about 'law' and 'rights' and even worshipped secretly. Their senior officers regularly stood up to the Japanese authorities, even though the consequences were usually painful and sometimes fatal.

General Percival issued a directive to all the prisoners at Changi Prisoner of War Camp that reaffirmed the duty of every soldier to attempt to escape, but cautioned the men that they should only attempt to do so after proper planning had been conducted, and the chances of actually getting away appeared good. Percival knew, as most Allied prisoners knew, that the chances of reaching Allied lines were virtually nil, and once a prisoner had stepped through the wire he was on borrowed time. Simply throwing away lives in pointless escapes was not acceptable to Percival when even basic survival inside the camps was extremely precarious. 'We had to adjust our actions accordingly,' wrote Percival. 'There is nothing to be gained in such circumstances in being obstinate.'[3]

The attitude of the Japanese to escape attempts, though not yet formalised, was, judging by their general demeanour towards POWs, harsh and bloody. Some men did try to get away from Singapore, but it was incredibly difficult. They were on an island infested by Japanese, deep within Japanese controlled territory, they were white and they could not count on assistance from the civilian population. The Chinese were pro-British to a certain extent, but terrified of the Japanese after the bestial Sook Ching Massacre after the fall of the island, when the Japanese had machine-gunned thousands on the beaches. While many Chinese remained loyal to Britain, many Malays and Indians were openly hostile to their former colonial masters, and they were being actively courted by the Japanese, who were encouraging the spread of anti-colonial nationalist movements within the territories they had occupied and even trying to form quisling foreign legions such as the Indian National Army.

At Changi, Lieutenant Colonel Charles Heath, commanding officer of 9th Coast Regiment, Royal Artillery, was forced to witness the execution of three of his men for attempting to escape in March 1942, around the same time that Acting Corporal Breavington and Private Gale were planning their quest for freedom. On 19 March 1942 Heath was summoned to General Percival's headquarters inside the camp, and informed that three young soldiers from his regiment, Gunners D. Hunter, J. McCann and G. Jeffries, 'had been apprehended by the Japanese outside the camp and that the Japanese proposed to shoot them. I went to Headquarters ... where I was told by Brigadier [Terence] Newbigging that the Japanese were determined to carry out the shooting despite the fact that General Percival had lodged a strong protest against it as being absolutely illegal.'[4] Newbigging decided to go and see Lieutenant Okasaki, Supervising Officer at the Japanese Prisoner of War Administration office at Changi. Joining him for the short drive were Heath, Captain B. Griffith, the condemned men's battery commander, and Padre Watson. As Newbigging pulled in at the Japanese HQ a truck pulled up with the three British gunners loaded aboard. Newbigging spoke to Okasaki at some length, but made no progress. He turned to Heath and told him that the Japanese had rejected Percival's plea of leniency and they were going to shoot the prisoners.

The officers drove behind the lorry, following it to a quiet beach. On the beach they discovered that the Japanese had dug a large single grave in the sand. Heath and his companions spoke to the three men, but what they said Heath did not record. The Japanese guards led the bound men to the edge of the grave. 'They were blindfolded and made to kneel down beside the grave at intervals of about one and a half yards. The Japanese firing party of three stood about thirty yards away and fired a volley on an order from the Japanese warrant officer or NCO in charge of

11

them. All three men fell almost simultaneously but not all of them were dead. The firing party and the NCO then walked up to the grave and ... finished off the prisoners still alive by firing at least 3 more shots.'[5] Afterwards, the Japanese soldiers filled the grave in, saluted, and placed some shrubs on the pile of sand in place of a wreath or flowers. The Japanese interpreter present turned to Heath and told him to warn his men 'that their fate would be the same if any of them were caught trying to escape.'[6]

At this stage there was no formal Japanese policy concerning the punishment for escapers, but the executions witnessed by Heath were obviously designed to prevent any further attempts at Changi. In this they failed.

Acting Corporal Breavington and Private Gale, the two Australians executed on the beach alongside two British soldiers on 2 September 1942, had made their escape attempt from Singapore two months after Gunners Hunter, McCann and Jeffries had been put to death. Breavington, in civilian life a police sergeant from Northcote, and Gale, a 23-year-old from Toronto, New South Wales, serving with Breavington in the 2/10th Ordnance Work- shop Company, RAAOC, managed to seize an open native fishing boat. They spent around six weeks at sea with minimal supplies, rowing and drifting several hundred miles before beaching on an Indonesian island where they were promptly recaptured. On 12 July 1942 both men had been admitted to Changi Military Hospital suffering from starvation and tropical diseases, Gale recovering more quickly than the older Breavington. The fact that the Japanese sent them to hospital indicates that they were unsure of how to punish them at this stage. In the case of Gunners Hunter, McCann and Jeffries in March 1942, the Japanese had shot all three men for the 'crime' of attempted escape.

Once Breavington and Gale were fit they were discharged back into Changi Camp. It was at this point, in August 1942, that the Japanese decreed all Allied POWs must sign a document, which read: 'I hereby, on my honour, promise that I will not attempt to escape.'[7] The penalty for breaching this contract was, un- surprisingly, death. Senior Allied officers were appalled by this breach of the accepted Rules of War, not to mention The Hague and Geneva Conventions, and they told their men not to sign.

The Japanese use of 'non-escape pledges' and similar good conduct documents requiring the signatures of POWs was unique in the history of warfare. It revealed that the Japanese military wished to formalise its regulations for POWs concerning escape by making prisoners responsible for their own illegal ill treatment and murder. The documents served to remove from POWs their internationally recognised legal protections under the Rules of War and to replace them with a set of completely arbitrary regulations that could be applied according to the whims of Japanese commanders rather than through any real legal process. The Japanese also revealed the cynical nature of their requests by often breaking their word in agreements with Allied POWs, and in denying prisoners any due process of military law, even Japanese military law, in cases of escape or overt resistance to Japanese regulations.

Major General Hervey Sitwell, commanding British forces on Java, surrendered on 12 March 1942 to Lieutenant General Maruyama of 2nd Imperial Guards Division. During the surrender negotiations General Sitwell recalled that both he and his RAF commander, Air Vice Marshal Paul Maltby, were specifically concerned about the application of the Geneva Conventions. 'When the terms were originally handed to Air Vice Marshal Maltby and myself, they were of unconditional surrender, and that all troops would obey absolutely any orders of the Japanese troops,'[8] remarked Sitwell. Both Sitwell and Maltby were cautious of signing any document without proper assurances. 'I, and I think Air Vice Marshal Maltby also, asked Maruyama through his interpreter whether that would mean we would have the benefit of the Geneva Convention.'[9] General Maruyama 'said that we should certainly have the benefit of the Geneva Convention, and accordingly a statement to this effect was included in the surrender terms.'[10] Sitwell and Maltby remained suspicious and they demanded further written assurances from Maruyama. 'Maltby suggested that the word "lawful" should be inserted before the word "orders", but the Japanese refused to insert this word, arguing that no orders given by the Japanese would be illegal, and further that we were completely covered against illegal orders by the promise that the conditions of the Geneva Convention would be fulfilled.'[11] We can perhaps suggest that Sitwell and Maltby were naïve or overly trusting, as it was well known that the Japanese had rejected the Geneva Conventions in other wars, but in such a position the Allied leaders had to try and obtain the best treatment possible for their men.

General Sitwell discovered that the Japanese were barefaced liars just eight days after signing the surrender document when he was brutally interrogated for military information in direct violation of the Geneva Conventions. On 20 March 1942 Sitwell was taken before a Major Saito of the *Kempeitai* Military Police in Bandoeng. Saito was described by Sitwell as 'very dark; wore spectacles; very Japanese in appearance; rather a projecting jaw; had a most villainous face.' Sitwell recalled in 1945, 'He asked me a number of questions which I refused to answer, the upshot of which was that Saitu [sic] said I must answer and that I was only a prisoner. He then threatened me and said that it would cost me my life if I did not answer.'[12] Sitwell thought that Saito was bluffing. 'I said that under the Geneva Convention he could not make use of threats. His answer to this was that Japan only stuck to the Geneva Convention when it suited her the same as Britain did. I got angry at this and turned my back on Saitu, whereupon he gave an order to the guard and I was taken outside.'[13] The 46-year-old British Major General was frogmarched to a grubby concrete cell, 'where I was handed over to about five dirty Japanese who were in uniform ... They proceeded to beat me up with their hands and boots, kicking me in the ribs frequently and about the head.' Some of the guards even stamped on Sitwell's head, the others 'endeavoured to remove my badges of rank which I was wearing, and I was eventually knocked unconscious.'[14] Following this assault, Sitwell endured eighteen days of solitary confinement; much of it bound up and forced to sit on the floor. If the Japanese could treat a captured general in this fashion, their attitude towards junior officers and other ranks would be easy to guess.

In July 1942 the Japanese authorities at Bicycle Camp in Java ordered all British, Australian, American and Dutch prisoners to sign a form promising that they would obey all orders of the Imperial Japanese Army, including not attempting to escape. The prisoners discussed the wording of the pledge and they demanded that the phrase 'subject to the oath of allegiance I have already taken' be added to the document as a disclaimer before they would sign it. This decision was unanimous, and the reaction of the Japanese was predictable intransigence followed swiftly by threats and violence.

On 3 July the two senior Allied officers at the camp, Brigadier Arthur Blackburn, Australian holder of the Victoria Cross, and Colonel A.C. Searle, US Army, told the camp commandant that if the phrase was added, all of the prisoners would sign the form. It seemed like a reasonable compromise to the Allied officers. However, the word 'reasonable' was not in the vocabulary of most Japanese officers. The commandant, keen neither to lose face nor to be 'advised' by his slaves, dug in his heels and insisted that all the POWs sign the form in its original wording. The commandant decided to make his intention perfectly clear and ordered his guards to beat up large numbers of Allied POWs that afternoon, leaving many in the hospital. Brigadier Blackburn was taken to the Japanese headquarters in Batavia where a staff officer bluntly warned him that unless all of the prisoners signed the form, the camp's supplies of food and medicines, which were already barely able to sustain life, would be 'progressively reduced.'[15] In cases like these, going head-to-head with Japanese commandants always resulted in appalling violence. The issue of 'face' was barely understood by most Allied POWs, senior officers included, in much the same way that the commandants did not understand the POWs insistence on their rights and privileges. The two sides may have come from different planets rather than different countries such were the mistrust and confusion between them.

At dawn on 4 July the POWs inside Bicycle Camp watched teams of Japanese guards setting up light machine guns around the camp perimeter. Then a notice appeared on the main notice board that bluntly stated that the lives of the prisoners could no longer be guaranteed. The commandant then ordered that Brigadier Blackburn and Colonel Searle be placed under arrest. If the commandant had compromised he would have lost face in front of his subordinates and appeared weak – therefore in order to maintain his position and the respect of his men he had to push the issue as far as possible in the hope that the POWs would relent in a face-saving climb-down. Picking on the ringleaders of the resistance, Blackburn and Searle, had the desired effect because both senior officers were genuinely concerned for the lives of their men. As Blackburn was being marched to the guardhouse he managed to yell out orders to his men, telling them to sign the form and not to resist the Japanese any further.

The commandant's final gambit was to remove all of the Allied officers from the camp. He thought that the officers had ordered their men not to sign his pledge and so he ordered the officers paraded and then marched out of the camp. Once the officers were all gone, the Japanese guards, using rifle butts, wooden sticks and their boots, herded the other ranks into their huts where the forms awaited their signatures. Every man signed, as per Brigadier Blackburn's order. That evening Blackburn and Searle also signed the pledge. The commandant was satisfied but also very angry that his prisoners had dared to defy him, so he ordered his men to beat the prisoners again, many falling insensible to rifle butts and clubs. The beatings continued for a month until the commandant felt that his face and his authority had been sufficiently restored. Defiance was not permitted in Japanese prison camps. For example, every Allied prisoner, regardless of rank, had to bow to and salute every Japanese guard that they encountered in direct violation of law and military custom. This was because in the Japanese military mentality the lowliest private was superior to a surrendered lieutenant general. One was a soldier, the other a shameful non-entity. If the private viciously beat the general for not saluting it was no more of an offence than if he was to beat a recalcitrant dog. Japanese prisoner of war camps were a long way from the likes of Colditz Castle.

In Hong Kong, the first British territory to fall to the Japanese on Christmas Day 1941, the local commander of POWs, the odious, obese and corrupt Lieutenant Colonel Isao Tokunaga, strong-armed resistant Allied prisoners into signing escape pledges. 'Fat Pig' Tokunaga, as he was known among the prisoners, explained to them that since the surrender of Hong Kong had been un-conditional every prisoner must sign the document. The prisoners faced exactly the same choice as that offered by the Japanese authorities in Singapore and Java – either sign the illegal docu-ment, or face punishment. Tokunaga boldly declared to assembled Canadian POWs at North Point Camp on 23 May 1942 that failure to sign the pledge would signify 'mutiny for which death was the obvious outcome.'[16]

British and Canadian officers and men initially stood their ground against Tokunaga, explaining forcefully that it was their duty as POWs to attempt to escape, and that the Japanese document was illegal and in contravention of the Rules of War. The same argument was faced by the Japanese every time they introduced their pledge papers. But the Japanese simply segregated the troublesome prisoners and attempted to bribe them into signing by feeding them large portions of hot food, steaming mugs of tea and cigarettes. Most relented when they realised that the Japanese document had no grounding in law and signing it under duress rendered it meaningless. A hard core of soldiers held out on strongly held principles and paid a heavy price. The Japanese quickly realised that such men would not listen to reason, neither were they susceptible to bribery, so they fell back on their *modus operandi* – violence. The Japanese beat the recalcitrant Canadian POWs at North Point with whips, canes and bats, and six of them were taken to Stanley Prison where they were woken up every hour throughout the night and severely beaten with truncheons. In between pastings their Japanese torturers urged them to sign the pledge. But even constant assault and battery did not break the hard-core resisters' will, so on 31 May 1942 their food and water was stopped. Realising that the Japanese meant to obtain their signatures or murder them in the process, the six prisoners, in order to save their own lives, reluctantly signed on 4 June.

The Japanese were prepared to stoop very low indeed when it came to forcing POWs to sign their infernal non-escape pledges. Lieutenant Colonel Tokunaga insisted that as well as 'healthy' prisoners in the Hong Kong camps, the sick and wounded at Bowen Road Military Hospital would also have to sign. Tokunaga, taking no chances this time, decided to begin his request with a shocking display of callousness and disregard for human life. On 26 May 1942 all of the patients were carried out of their beds and placed on the hospital tennis courts, along with all of the British medical staff, and there left under the boiling hot sun without a drop of water for the rest of the day. In the late afternoon a British officer arrived from Argyle Street Officer's Camp and informed the patients and medics that Major General Christopher Maltby, former commander of the Hong Kong garrison, felt that they ought to sign the document to avoid further needless suffering – most did so and were returned to the hospital. Maltby and other senior officers felt that the contents of the document were null and void anyway, as the POWs had only signed under extreme duress. This was a line taken by all senior POWs throughout the Japanese prison camp system. The pattern was eerily similar at each location. When presented with the ludicrous non-escape pledge the officers bravely raised strong objections. The Japanese predictably became enraged that mere 'slaves' had the presumption to question their wisdom and violently intimidated the POWs. Senior Allied officers then instructed their men to sign after it became clear that the Japanese would stop at nothing to get their way, including torture and murder. Mass punishment appears to have been the favoured Japanese reaction to POW resistance, and the most infamous mass punishment occurred in Singapore.

At Changi Camp on Singapore Island the commandant decided upon a different, though no less ghastly, approach to getting his way over the issue of the non-escape pledge. At the end of August 1942 he ordered that 15,000 British and Australian POWs be moved into Selarang Barracks within the Changi Cantonment. The order soon had all the makings of a serious humanitarian disaster. Selarang Barracks, built in 1936–38, was designed to house in peacetime between 800 and 1,200 soldiers. It consisted of seven barrack blocks constructed around a central parade square and before the war had been the garrison for 2nd Battalion, Gordon Highlanders. The overcrowding caused by the Japanese order was immense, with a tent city springing up across the previously immaculate parade square. The Japanese turned the screw further when they ordered the water to the toilets to be shut off. Allied officers ordered that latrines be dug on the square. The POWs were only allowed one quart of water per day for each man to drink and wash in as the Japanese left the 15,000 men just two water taps. On the first day thirty-five men had gone down with dysentery, on the second day eighty and by the third the medical officers had given up counting.

Because Breavington, Gale, Waters and Fletcher had escaped before the non-escape pledge had been promulgated senior Allied officers believed that the death penalty did not apply to these men. But the Japanese viewed their own rules in a completely flexible way and instead they ordered that the four escapers be retroactively put to death in order to persuade the remaining prisoners of their willingness to enforce their new regulation, not to mention the punishment for not signing the pledge. After three days of appalling overcrowding at Selarang had failed to break the prisoners' resolve the Japanese ordered the executions to be carried out. Breavington had pleaded with the Japanese to spare Private Gale, saying that the younger soldier had only been following his orders, but it made no difference. On 5 September, three days after the four men had been shot and buried on Changi Beach, General Percival ordered that all prisoners sign the non-escape pledge. Percival and his officers viewed the non-escape pledge as carrying no legality whatsoever. Signing satisfied the Japanese and they permitted the men at Selarang to return to their previous accommodation, thereby saving innumerable lives.

From now on, escaping from the Japanese had become a very dangerous game indeed. If recaptured, an escaper could expect no mercy. In one horrific, though by no means unique, example Private John Simpson of the Border Regiment was recaptured after an unsuccessful escape attempt from Changi. The Japanese beat him severely and then cut out his tongue. But they didn't kill him, indicating once more the completely arbitrary application of Japanese regulations. On repatriation to England after the war Simpson became a recluse and eventually committed suicide, and he was not alone in such a tragic fate. The Japanese would go to extreme lengths to make examples of such brave men, and few were given the kind of relatively clean and quick deaths given to Breavington, Gale, Waters and Fletcher on 2 September 1942.

Acting Corporal Breavington was posthumously Mentioned in Despatches. In March 2011 the Australian government honoured all twenty of their servicemen, including Breavington and Gale, who were killed escaping from Japanese captivity during the war, each man receiving a Commendation for Gallantry, the modern Australian equivalent to being Mentioned in Despatches. (As yet, the British government has no plans to do the same for the British soldiers who were executed for attempting to escape.)

The new non-escape pledge was ruthlessly applied on the Burma-Thailand Railway, the great Japanese military engineering feat that was completed over the bodies of hundreds of thousands of British, Australian, Dutch, American and native prisoners. The most famous example was that of the 'Tavoy Eight'.[17] In May 1942 a large consignment of POWs from Changi known as 'A' Force under the command of Australian Brigadier Arthur Varley had been shipped to Thailand aboard two rusting, dilapidated 'hell ships'. A dysentery outbreak weakened hundreds of Australian prisoners before they even began work. Split into three working parties, some men looked for a way out. Eight members of the 4th Anti-Tank Regiment, Royal Australian Artillery, led by Warrant Officer Class 2 Matthew Quittenton, did just that and escaped into the jungle at Tavoy, Burma. Unfortunately they were swiftly recaptured and four days later sentenced to death by firing squad. Brigadier Varley was forced to witness the execution of the Tavoy Eight. He recorded in his diary the incredible bravery that Quittenton and his men exhibited as the sixteen-man Japanese firing squad formed up in front of them. 'The spirit of these eight Australians was wonderful. They spoke cheerios and good luck messages to one another, and never showed any sign of fear. A truly courageous end.'[18]

Such then was the Japanese 'policy', but both before and after its promulgation there were many gallant escapes, some of which succeeded. We need to go back to Hong Kong for the first – a daring escape by a rag-tag assortment of British military and civilians in the face of the Japanese invasion and their truly incredible trek through Occupied China to freedom. The story reveals that many escapers could rely upon some assistance from Allied intelligence organisations and local guerrilla networks. These are often the unsung heroes of the story of the escapes, the men and women, often locals, who risked their lives to help strangers.

Chapter 2

Fast Boat to China

All the time I could see the familiar sites, the Peak houses, the Aberdeen Rd, the famous fish restaurants on the corner where I had eaten many lunches; and all the time the Japanese machine gunners on the hillsides 600 yards away went for us hammer and tongs.

David MacDougall,
Ministry of Information, Hong Kong

Sleek grey motor torpedo boats sat gently bobbing against a wooden jetty, their superstructures draped with camouflage netting and recently cut foliage in an attempt to make them appear to be just an extension of the jungle-covered island to which they were moored. The effect had worked, for although Japanese aircraft had occasionally buzzed overhead, no bombs had fallen. The crews worked feverishly to load the MTBs with stores, fuel and weapons for the coming journey while ashore officers listened to the sounds of heavy fighting in the far distance, the crump of artillery and mortars mixed with the crackle of machine guns and rifles. Columns of smoke rose on the horizon from the direction of Hong Kong Island and Kowloon. 'How much longer?' was the most common comment that passed between officers and men, as well as 'will they make it?' The MTBs were hidden for one specific reason – to make possible the escape from doomed Hong Kong of a very special group of Allied officers who must, under no circumstances, fall into the hands of the Japanese. So wait the

21

crews must, biting their fingernails and constantly scanning the surrounding water and islands with binoculars for some sign of the promised passengers.

The task of defending the indefensible British colony of Hong Kong had been given to the army in 1940. The garrison troops were drawn from Britain, Canada and India supported by local Chinese and European volunteer forces. The Royal Air Force had practically ceased to exist as a presence in China, having only three elderly Vickers Vildebeest torpedo bombers and a pair of Supermarine Walrus maritime patrol aircraft stationed at RAF Kai Tak in Hong Kong. The Japanese destroyed both seaplanes and two of the torpedo bombers on the first day of the battle on 8 December 1941, and also destroyed or damaged most of the civilian aircraft being employed by the Air Section of the Hong Kong Volunteer Defence Corps. Major General Christopher Maltby, the British commander, tried to slow the Japanese assault by falling back onto prepared defensive positions in the New Territories, particularly a line of redoubts and trench systems called the Gin Drinker's Line. But Maltby's 10,000 Commonwealth and Empire troops were heavily outnumbered by the combat-experienced 50,000 men of the Japanese 38th Division, and many, including the Canadians, had only recently arrived in the colony and lacked any combat experience. The British did not expect to be able to prevent the Japanese from taking Hong Kong, and instead Maltby had been ordered by Churchill to delay the inevitable for as long as possible, fighting a protracted battle from the mainland onto the island itself before surrendering. British resistance in indefensible Hong Kong was vital to buy more time for the defence of the Malayan Peninsula and the strategic naval base at Singapore. But Maltby's attempt to follow a Maginot Line-strategy was doomed to failure.

Elsewhere, British military prestige in China had sunk to a very low ebb. Shanghai, once a major base for British military forces, had, by December 1941, been largely abandoned to the Japanese. HMS *Peterel* was the first of the remaining Royal Navy vessels in China to be destroyed by the Japanese, and the first shots fired in anger between British and Japanese forces occurred in downtown Shanghai.

The *Peterel* had been in the service of the Royal Navy since 1927, when she had emerged with her sister-ship, HMS *Gannet*, from the yard of Yarrow & Co. Ltd, England, and been shipped in pieces to China. Since the end of the nineteenth century the Royal Navy had patrolled the Yangtze River in various classes of gunboats, maintaining, along with the other nations who had successfully crushed the Boxer Rebellion in 1900, the right to police the river-borne trade of China, and to provide the Chinese with a visible symbol of western military power. The *Peterel* displaced 310 tons, and was armed with two 3-inch guns, and eight machine guns. But, on the morning the Second World War came to Shanghai her main guns had been immobilised some time before, and her normal ship's company of fifty-five men had been reduced to a skeleton crew of twenty as the vessel performed the role of a floating communication station for the nearby British Embassy under the command of a tough New Zealander, Lieutenant Stephen Polkinghorn of the Royal Naval Reserve.

Polkinghorn received a telephone call from the British Consulate informing him of the Japanese attack at Pearl Harbor, and he was advised that the Japanese were at war with Britain as well. *Peterel*'s commanding officer had his remaining crew ordered to 'battle stations' immediately. Also in Shanghai harbour that morning was an American warship, the gunboat USS *Wake*. In common with the *Peterel*, the *Wake* was also immobilised. At 4am Japanese troops came to take the surrender of both Allied ships. A boarding party quickly overwhelmed the *Wake* (for the full story see Chapter 7), and the Japanese captured the vessel intact and without firing a shot. Triumphant Japanese soldiers raised their national flag at the *Wake*'s stern, and she was later incorporated into the Imperial Japanese Navy as the *Tataru Maru*. The Royal Navy had already planned for such an eventuality concerning the *Peterel*, and the ship had been rigged with scuttling charges to prevent her capture. Although the *Peterel* was small, outdated and insignificant, naval honour dictated that no British ship would be handed intact to the enemy.

Polkinghorn allowed several Japanese officers to board the gunboat, as they wished to discuss the surrender of the *Peterel* and her crew. Polkinghorn, by his own admission, was playing for time, in order to give his crew time to set the charges that would send the vessel to the bottom of the Huangpu River. When the Japanese demanded he surrender his ship immediately, Polkinghorn ordered them to leave the *Peterel* with the famous words: 'Get off my bloody ship!' The Japanese cruiser *Izumo*, accompanied by a gunboat, opened fire on the British ship shortly afterwards. Hopelessly outgunned, the British sailors responded with only two operable machine guns, but the *Peterel* was soon reduced to a blazing wreck and began to drift clear of the dock. Polkinghorn gave the order to abandon ship, and the *Peterel* rolled over and sank. The crew were rounded up by the Japanese and taken prisoner, though the plucky New Zealand skipper was later awarded the Distinguished Service Cross for his gallant resistance.

Major General Maltby's only hope of holding the Japanese in Hong Kong was to inflict upon them a delaying action centred on the Shing Mun Redoubt, the Gin Drinker's Line's main defensive position. But Maltby could only spare a single platoon to defend the Redoubt against several Japanese regiments and it was easily captured on 10 December, forcing the British to abandon the entire length of their static fortifications in the New Territories. Maltby had hoped that the Gin Drinker's Line would have held the Japanese for at least two weeks.

On 11 December the Japanese began advancing into the city of Kowloon, with the British Mainland Brigade retreating quickly through the town under heavy artillery and aerial attack towards the ferry terminals to Hong Kong Island. Although the 7th Rajput Regiment bravely formed a rearguard that enabled most of the British and Indian troops to cross over to Hong Kong Island, the Japanese rapidly captured the town and the Royal Navy base. One of the final actions before the Japanese overran the naval base on 12 December was the scuttling of the headquarters vessel, the 3,650-ton HMS *Tamar*. The venerable wooden vessel, built in 1863, had served as China Station Headquarters since 1897.

That same day as the *Tamar* was being blown apart, HMS *Moth*, an Insect-class gunboat, was also lost when her dry dock was deliberately flooded. The twelve vessels of the Insect class had been constructed during the First World War for service against the Austro-Hungarian Danube Flotilla. Ironically, the class were ordered as 'China gunboats' to conceal their true destination, but eleven of them did eventually end up patrolling the rivers of China. Before being sunk in Hong Kong, *Moth* had patrolled the Yangtze River for many years, a powerful presence as the vessel was twice the size, at 645 tons, of the other classes of British gunboats, and well-armed. The Japanese later salvaged the *Moth* in July 1942, and she was commissioned as the *Suma* and sent back to patrolling the Yangtze. On 19 March 1945 she struck an American mine near Nanjing and sank.

The other Insect class gunboat present in Hong Kong during the battle, HMS *Cicala*, was in the thick of the action from the outset, and under repeated dive-bomber attack. The vessel's two 6-inch and two 12-pounder guns were backed up by a 3-inch anti-aircraft gun and six Lewis Machine Guns, and by violent manoeuvring and a near constant flak barrage the gunboat avoided serious damage until near the end of the battle.

In the meantime, what remained of the Royal Navy was ordered to vacate Hong Kong and make for the safety of the Singapore Naval Base. The Royal Navy's presence in Hong Kong had been steadily run down since the outbreak of war in Europe. The major vessels of the 5th Cruiser Squadron had all departed by the end of 1940 to where they would be usefully employed fighting the Germans, followed by the nine boats of the 4th Submarine Flotilla. When the order to evacuate Hong Kong was received following the Japanese invasion, two of the three destroyers stationed there left as quickly as possible. Only the Admiralty S-class destroyer HMS *Thracian* remained as Japanese air activity over the naval base and Victoria went unchecked by any fears of British fighter interdiction. This lone destroyer was now the navy's largest vessel in China and the remaining ships in Hong Kong harbour were either too small or too insignificant to be evacuated. There were six gunboats of assorted classes and sizes, nine auxiliary minesweepers and nine local defence craft, as well as the auxiliary patrol vessels HMS *Kai Ming* and *Swanley*. Elsewhere in China the Royal Navy had practically disappeared. Up the coast in Shanghai the gunboat HMS *Peterel* had been sunk. The only other commissioned Royal Navy ship in Shanghai was HMS *Ah Ming*, a tug. Three other gunboats, HMS *Gannet*, *Falcon* and *Sandpiper*, had gone deep inland away from Japanese activity and would in due course be turned over to the Chinese Nationalist Navy and their British crew evacuated overland to Burma.

On 13 December one of the small force of gunboats managed to score a victory for the British defence. HMS *Tern*, a 262-ton vessel built in England in 1927 downed a Japanese aircraft with her two 3-inch guns, one of the few successes recorded by the Royal Navy during the battle. The Japanese now settled into preparing for an amphibious assault across Victoria Harbour, and they extensively shelled and bombed the island's north shore to soften up its defences.

Grounding on Lamma Island on 15 December damaged HMS *Thracian* as she avoided repeated Japanese aerial attacks. The *Thracian*'s skipper, Lieutenant Commander A.L. Pears, decided on a drastic course of action. On the following night the badly damaged destroyer was deliberately run aground on Round Island in Repulse Bay in an effort to scuttle her. However, the attempt failed and the Japanese later captured the destroyer. Turned over to the Imperial Japanese Navy in November 1942 after extensive repairs, the *Thracian* was commissioned as Patrol Vessel 101, and was then made a training ship in 1944. She ended the war in Yokosuka, Japan, attached to the torpedo school before being captured by the Americans. Hauled back to Hong Kong, the destroyer was broken up shortly after the war.

There remained only one unit that still could pack a considerable offensive punch and that had been ordered to remain in Hong Kong because the small size of its vessels meant they could be effectively hidden around the colony, and their speed and firepower would prove very effective in disrupting a Japanese amphibious assault on Hong Kong Island from captured Kowloon. This was the 2nd Motor Torpedo Boat (MTB) Flotilla, formed in 1938 to bolster British defences in Hong Kong. In May 1941 Lieutenant Commander Gerard Gandy, who was a descendent of Admiral Lord Nelson, took over command of the vessels. Part-time seamen from the Hong Kong Royal Naval Volunteer Reserve replaced most of the Flotilla's professional Royal Navy officers, who returned to the shooting war in Europe.

The Flotilla was equipped with the British Power Boat 60-foot MTB designed in 1936. They had a top speed of 33 knots and were armed with two 18-inch torpedoes and five Lewis Machine Guns. After the departure of most Royal Navy blue-water assets in 1940, the MTBs remained the only real offensive vessels left to the British in China.

On 13 December MTBs *07* and *09* had performed sterling service evacuating troops of the 5/7th Rajputs from North Lyemun to the destroyer HMS *Thracian* waiting offshore after the Indian battalion had formed part of the Garrison's rearguard at Kowloon. The two MTBs had taken off 260 men from the devastated battalion, which had lost all of its British officers during the retreat from the Gin Drinker's Line.

On 18 December *MTB08* blew up on her slip at Aberdeen Island after a bomb splinter hit her during the incessant Japanese air attacks. Three days later the remaining boats of 2nd MTB Flotilla went into action as Japanese troops were being ferried across Victoria Harbour from Kowloon to Hong Kong Island in a daring amphibious assault. *MTB07*, under the command of Acting Petty Officer Buddy Hide, came under intense machine-gun, mortar and artillery fire off North Point, but Hide pressed home his attack with great courage and determination, managing to sink several Japanese landing craft. The MTB's Lewis Guns raked the Japanese vessels from end to end, and the backwash from the big engines overturned several, leaving enemy soldiers thrashing around in the water. Hide also dropped a few depth charges as *MTB07* powered through the Japanese flotilla like a lion through a herd of wildebeest. *MTB09* entered Kowloon Harbour tearing through the remnants of the landing craft Hide had already destroyed, peppering swimming Japanese with machine-gun fire, but hotly pursued by Japanese aircraft who were determined to sink her. Leading Stoker Reg Barker was mortally wounded and *MTB09*'s starboard engine was knocked out by aerial cannon fire. *MTB07* was raked by Japanese automatic fire, killing two of her crew. Both boats tried to extricate themselves at reduced speed, *MTB09* managing to hit two Japanese aircraft with its Lewis Guns. It had been a valiant effort against superior odds, and the MTB attacks undoubtedly caused some loss and disrupted the Japanese landings.

A second pair of boats, MTBs *11* and *12*, roared into Kowloon Harbour to finish off any remaining landing craft, but *MTB12* took a direct hit and smashed at full speed into the harbour wall – only three out of her crew of twelve survived the impact. *MTB11* made it back, and orders were given to stand the rest of the flotilla down. Unfortunately, *MTB26* missed this order and was last seen sitting motionless in the harbour with a single Lewis Gun firing madly. The operation to disrupt the Japanese landings had cost the lives of twenty British sailors, and caused the loss of two irreplaceable Motor Torpedo Boats. Only five boats remained seaworthy.

Although a brave gesture, the MTB attacks could not prevent the Japanese from landing in force on the north shore of Hong Kong Island. Three Japanese regiments came ashore on 18 December, and the final battle for Hong Kong commenced as General Maltby threw his remaining two brigades of infantry against the invaders. On 19 December fierce fighting raged throughout the island, but the Japanese successfully cut the British defences in two, and although the British forces bravely attempted to re-establish a defensive line the Japanese were too numerous and too strong. The gunboat HMS *Tern* was scuttled in Deep Water Bay, possibly as the result of a mistaken signal. On 21 December the gunboat *Cicala*, having stood off an amazing sixty Japanese dive-bomber attacks during the course of the battle, finally succumbed to the inevitable and was destroyed. Struck by three bombs in the West Lamma Channel close to Hong Kong Island, she was probably also scuttled.

The British lost control of the island's vital water reservoirs as the fighting progressed through the Wong Nei Chong Gap, and eighteen days after the initial Japanese attack across the Sham Chun River on the border, Maltby prepared reluctantly to surrender. The last of the gunboats was also scuttled on 25 December. HMS *Robin*, built in 1934 and one of the final gunboats dispatched to Chinese waters, disappeared beneath the waves to prevent her capture by the victorious Japanese.

With the surrender of the colony inevitable, the Commodore in Hong Kong, commanding all remaining naval assets, ordered all Royal Navy vessels except the MTBs and their tenders to scuttle themselves.

The decision had been taken, as per a pre-war agreement, that the remaining MTBs were to be used to evacuate the 46-year-old one-armed and one-legged Vice Admiral Chan Chak and his small Chinese Nationalist Navy liaison party from Hong Kong to prevent their capture by the Japanese. Admiral Chan had been in Hong Kong since 1938 assisting the Hong Kong Police and army intelligence. His cover was as a stockbroker for Wah Kee & Company in the Shell Building on Queen's Road. A small Chinese team assisted Chan. Colonel Yee Shui Kee of the Chinese Secret Service posed as an insurance salesman from Shanghai; Lieutenant Commander Henry Heng Hsu was Chan's flag commander; and Coxswain Yeung Chuan, a martial arts expert, acted as Chan's bodyguard. Admiral Chan was the Kuomintang leader for the entire region, and he had extensive contacts with Chinese guerrillas operating behind Japanese lines, making him doubly useful to the British now that defeat appeared a foregone conclusion.

The old Chinese criminal organisations called the Triads worked for the Japanese during the invasion of the New Territories and Kowloon. The Japanese *Kempeitai* Military Police paid them handsomely for their cooperation, and because of Triad sabotage activities the Imperial Army was able to overcome General Maltby's defences in only four days. Admiral Chan decided that he must prevent the same thing from occurring on Hong Kong Island. He decided to raise money from among the British and Chinese communities to out-pay the Japanese and gain the services of the Triads. This ploy worked, as the Triads were basically opportunists who would work for anyone willing to pay well. The Triads and the British Special Operations Executive (SOE) team worked together to eliminate the dangerous Japanese Fifth Column that was threatening the rear areas in Hong Kong before the Japanese crossed the harbour. Those suspected Fifth Columnists were rounded up and summarily shot by Punjabi troops.

SOE's Z Force consisted of Mike Kendall, Major Colin McEwan and Monia (John) Talan. McEwan was a former Edinburgh University rugby blue and HKVDC officer, while Talan was a White Russian émigré who had been working in Hong Kong when the war broke out.

On 20 December orders were received by the 2nd MTB Flotilla to break out to Mainland China, and in the event of not reaching

Allied lines, to act as a guerrilla force until relieved by an allegedly advancing Chinese Nationalist army. The next day the three-man SOE team arrived and loaded *MTB10* with Bren guns, explosives, food and clothing. Coming along for the ride were four officers from General Maltby's Battlebox headquarters. They had asked for permission to attempt to break out instead of surrendering, and Maltby had freely given them leave to do so. They were Major Arthur Goring of 11th King Edward's Own Lancers (Probyn's Horse), RAF Squadron Leader Maxwell Oxford and Police Super-intendent William Robinson of the Indian Intelligence Bureau. The first two would have been extremely valuable to the *Kempeitai*, and it was imperative that they were not captured. 'Three or four days before the end we were under official orders to get away at the last moment at all costs after picking up the official party,' wrote Lieutenant Ron Ashby, an MTB commander.[1]

The remaining seaworthy MTBs were loaded with iron rations, rifles, stores and equipment. Kendall and his team also had time to brief the matelots on behind-the-lines survival techniques. In order to preserve the vessels ready for the escape, the boats were hidden out of harm's way. MTBs *07* and *09* were tied up along a pier in Telegraph Bay between Mount Davis and Aberdeen, the crews carefully camouflaging the vessels against Japanese aircraft with straw, canvas and tree branches. MTBs *10*, *11* and *27* were hidden at the southwest tip of Ap Lei Chan, covering the exit to Aberdeen Harbour.

On 25 December the crews managed a reasonable Christmas dinner with a double ration of rum for each man. A ceasefire was called by the Japanese at 9am and lasted until noon as delegates from both sides discussed a British surrender. However, at noon the Japanese bombardment resumed. At 3pm, General Maltby advised the Governor, Sir Mark Young, that further useful military resistance was no longer possible. The British had been pushed back into the Stanley Peninsula. At 3.15pm Young informed the Japanese that the British would surrender, the final ceremony being conducted at the Peninsula Hotel in Kowloon at 6pm that evening. The Chinese dubbed the 25 December 1941 'Black Christmas' with good reason.

'I received a phone call from the battle box telling me that the back office is doing something and the meeting between departmental heads has been cancelled,' wrote Admiral Chan. 'Wait for the Governor's phone call at 3.00 pm. At this moment I knew that the future of HK was over.' Fortress HQ formally transferred command of the 2nd MTB Flotilla to Admiral Chan on the same day so that the officers and men would not be bound by the terms of the surrender. For the first time, British military personnel found themselves under Chinese command. Chan was widely respected, and everyone involved in the breakout knew that his contacts among the local guerrillas could mean the difference between freedom and capture in the days ahead.

At 3.45pm Canadian Ted Ross and his colleague David Mac-Dougall, who were both employees of the Ministry of Information, moved to King's Theatre from their office where they had orders to locate a large Buick car that had been parked there ready to take Admiral Chan's party to Aberdeen and the MTBs. At this point five staff officers arrived from Maltby's HQ, including Goring, Oxford and Robinson. The other two were Captain Peter Macmillan and Captain Freddie Guest, who was from The Middlesex Regiment. They quickly collected the Chinese party. When informed of the British surrender, Ross and MacDougall from the Ministry of Information immediately threw their lot in with Admiral Chan, and MacDougall armed himself with a revolver. 'Everywhere were signs of cast-off badges of office of all kinds: armbands of all descriptions of volunteer work; A.R.P., Special Police, Ambulance Badges, tin hats by the dozen and plenty of gas masks,' recalled Captain Guest. 'The Admiral was in ordinary Chinese clothes and carried a very small holdall with him. Macmillan and myself both still wore British uniform and carried just a few things we had been able to lay our hands on, in our pockets.'[2] They collected a canvas-topped Austin and then with the Buick following the two cars sped down a deserted Queen's Road. 'The British Army sentries at Queen Mary's Hospital were still in position,' noted Chan.

The main problem facing the Chan party was actually getting safely to the rendezvous with the MTBs hidden near Aberdeen. They were not the only military personnel who were determined to escape from the Japanese. At Staunton Creek they encountered the resourceful Commander Hugh Montague, who was over-seeing the refloating of Admiralty diesel launch *C-410* and the scuttling of the river gunboat HMS *Robin*. Montague intended to use the *C-410* to escape from Hong Kong, and Chan briefed him on the intended destination of the MTBs. Nearby, a party of sailors was trying to get HMS *Cornflower*'s launch going. The *Cornflower* was a 1,250-ton Arabis-class minesweeping corvette commissioned in 1916 that was scuttled in Hong Kong on 19 December. Christened 'Cornflower II', the vessel's cabin launch was big enough to accommodate the 16-man escaping party and take them to the MTBs. But the launch was without fuel and a charged battery. A rating dashed off in the Buick to the nearby naval stores and managed to procure 16 gallons of petrol. The Buick's battery managed to get the *Cornflower II*'s engine started. The boat was quickly filled with food, water and rifles, and the cars were abandoned. At 4.45pm the *Cornflower II* got underway, leaving Montague and his party still feverishly working on the *C-410*.

With Sub-Lieutenant Jacob Forster as skipper, Major Goring took overall charge aboard the overcrowded *Cornflower II* as the vessel weaved among the junks and wrecks that littered Aberdeen Harbour. The launch crept down the South Channel. Unfortunately, the *Cornflower II* was spotted by some four-dozen Japanese infantrymen who had just occupied a pillbox 200 yards away across the water on the mainland side. They immediately opened up a brisk fire with their rifles and two light machine guns. The launch was riddled from stem to stern. 'Well, we hadn't gone much more than five or six hundred yards when we were spotted from the shore and the Japs let fly at us with everything they had, rifles, machine guns and small shells,' recalled Ted Ross. 'The bullets simply whizzed through the side of the boat as if there had been no side there at all. Several of our chaps were hit, and soon a shot put the engine out of commission, that capped it. There we were, just sitting like ducks on a pond. The machine-gun bullets kept tearing in.'[3] Forster was struck in the stomach. Second Engineering Officer D. Harley, a Merchant Service officer from the SS *Yatshing*, went overboard and tried to swim to shore. 'A little behind me a man drowned noisily,' recalled McDougall. 'He took a long time to go down and I could do nothing about it.' MacDougall himself was wounded shortly afterwards. 'Mac got one right in his tin hat, another through the sole of his shoe, and just as he was saying how close they were coming he got one right in the back.'[4] The drifting *Cornflower II* was abandoned in the East Lamma Channel.

Some of the survivors swam to a nearby islet called Ap Lei Pai, while some struck out for Aberdeen Island. Commander Hsu helped Admiral Chan remove his clothes and false leg that contained HK$40,000. The leg and the money were abandoned, and the two Chinese officers went over the side of the riddled launch, taking shelter from the Japanese gunfire on the lee side. 'What should we do?' shouted Chan above the din to Hsu. 'Pray, pray to God,' replied the Christian Hsu. 'If we make it out of here, I'll convert to be a Christian,'[5] replied the Admiral. Missing an arm and a leg meant that Admiral Chan resorted to a strange lop-side crawl through the water. Initially Hsu, the current Hong Kong freestyle swimming champion, carried Chan on his back until the two became separated.

Ted Ross divested himself of his clothes, weapon and HK$2,000 before leaving the *Cornflower II*. 'Taking my clothes off made a whale of a difference! I was one of the last off the boat, but the first to reach the island. The water was dancing with bullets ... I dived and swam as far as I could under water, and finally got to the partial shelter of a rock on the shore.'[6] The Japanese continued to fire at the survivors as they dragged themselves ashore. MacDougall managed to swim to Ap Lei Pai Islet fully clothed and with his revolver still strapped around his waist. 'All the time I could see the familiar sites,' recalled MacDougall, 'the Peak houses, the Aberdeen Rd, the famous fish restaurants on the corner where I had eaten many lunches; and all the time the Japanese machine gunners on the hillsides 600 yards away went for us hammer and tongs.'[7] Ap Lei Pai was soon on fire as the Japanese lobbed phosphorous mortar bombs onto it, setting fire to the scrub vegetation.

At sunset, the survivors on the islet crossed the narrow isthmus to Aberdeen Island. Three boats of the 2nd MTB Flotilla were watching the exit from Aberdeen Harbour and awaiting the arrival of the survivors. A skiff containing Lieutenant Commander Yorath of the naval staff and Mr Halliday, a Merchant Navy engineer, arrived shortly before the *Cornflower II* survivors were located. Yorath passed on a verbal order from headquarters for the MTBs to proceed with their escape from Hong Kong immediately. The survivors were swimming and clambering along the rock shoreline towards the MTBs. Admiral Chan had been left behind and hidden among some rocks, while Hsu and the others went ahead to fetch some help. Able Seaman Downey at the MTBs was ordered to accompany Hsu in an open boat to search for and recover the Admiral. They sailed into the teeth of the enemy fire but could not locate Chan. They returned and collected more men, Commander Yorath and Bill Robinson volunteering to go with them. The party eventually located the Admiral by whistling into the darkness. 'The Admiral was practically at the top of the hill, although it was a difficult climb,' related Yorath. 'I think he must have gone up there to die – Chinese like having their graves on hillsides. As we rowed back, he sat facing me in the stern and crossed himself which rather surprised me.'[8]

Colonel Yee from Chan's staff became separated from his fellow countrymen and ended up ashore on Aberdeen Island with a Danish merchantman called Damsgaard and the wounded Forster. This trio hid in a church for a few days until Yee bribed a local to take the two wounded white men over to Hong Kong Island in his junk, where they were taken to hospital. Unfortunately, Forster was too badly injured and succumbed to his wounds. Damsgaard was sent to Stanley Civilian Interment Camp. Yee managed to avoid capture and made his own way to Chongqing and freedom.

Of the sixteen men who had started out aboard the *Cornflower II*, twelve made it to the concealed MTBs. There they were issued with dry clothes, steaming mugs of cocoa and tots of rum by the cheerful crews. The next problem was where to go. The MTBs were badly beaten up after seeing so much action since the Japanese invasion and their engines were in urgent need of maintenance. In consultation with the MTBs' officers, Admiral Chan decided on a relatively short journey north up the coast to Mirs Bay where Chan had excellent contacts among the local guerrillas.

In the meantime, Lieutenant Pittendrigh had managed to refloat Admiralty Launch *C-410*. Commander Hugh Montague decided to escape with a handful of men, his intention being to rendezvous with Chan's party in Mirs Bay and make his way to freedom on foot. At 7pm *C-410* left Aberdeen Harbour and proceeded to

Lamma Island, passed North-East Head and set course for Nan Ao Village in Mirs Bay where Montague hoped to find Admiral Chan and the Chinese guerrillas.

With Chan on the bridge of the leading MTB, the small flotilla powered out into East Lamma Channel at 9.40pm, the noise of the big engines deafening and more than living up to their Chinese nickname 'Wind Thunder Boats'. As the MTBs worked up to 22 knots on the calm water they encountered a Japanese cruiser that lobbed a handful of shells at them without result. The MTBs slipped past at high speed and arrived at Tung Ping Chau Island in Guangdong Province at 1.30am on 26 December. The boats anchored and Mike Kendall, along with his two SOE agents armed with Thompson sub-machine guns, and Lieutenant Commander Henry Hsu went ashore in two skiffs to make contact with the frightened locals, who initially thought that the MTBs were Japanese gunboats. After establishing contact with the village headman, they brought him aboard Chan's MTB for a meeting. The MTBs then motored to tiny Nan Ao Village on the Dapeng Peninsula and dropped anchor for a final time.

The searchlight of the Japanese cruiser also speared Commander Montague and the C-410, but inexplicably the Japanese held their fire and the launch was able to escape unscathed. Montague was so exhausted by the day's hectic escape and the enormous stress that he was under that he fell asleep at the helm and ran the C-410 aground in a bay near Nan Ao. All of the vessels were unloaded of their weapons, ammunition, supplies and loose gear. In January 1942, Kendall's Z Force retrieved the Lewis Guns and ammunition that were hidden in the village.

The escapees had managed to escape from Hong Kong, but they were still deep behind Japanese lines and they faced a long, arduous and very perilous journey to freedom. Their journey was only possible because of the assistance of Chinese guerrillas who were allied with Admiral Chan's Kuomintang government in Chongqing.

The escape party numbered sixty-eight men and one dog, Commander Collingwood's 'Bruce'. Mike Kendall took charge. A notorious Chinese smuggler and guerrilla named Leung Wing Yuen and his band of cutthroats would provide guides to move the British party into Chinese Nationalist territory. Sub-Lieutenant

Legge, who spoke fluent Cantonese, worked as a go-between along-side Admiral Chan and the Chinese guerrillas. Unfortunately, Chan realised that the MTBs and the admiralty launch would have to be abandoned, as the escapees would need to move inland on foot, initially to the Chinese stronghold at Waichow (now Huizhou) in the Pearl River Delta. Although Commander Collingwood protested, Chan ordered that the boats be scuttled. Skeleton crews backed the boats out a few hundred yards into deeper water and began the process of sinking them. 'We had to use axes on the wooden hulls, and open the sea cocks to let the water in,' recalled a British officer. 'The Chinese villagers piled rocks on board.'[9] The water was shallow enough that when the MTBs sank the tops of their bridges and the twelve-foot-high communications mast was visible, sticking up above the water (after the British had left a group of guerrillas chopped the masts down).

Admiral Chan's group was now deep behind enemy lines. They would have to walk to freedom, and for the largely unfit sailors who suddenly found themselves yomping over jungle-covered hills and mountains loaded down with rifles, machine guns, ammunition and personal kit, it was a daunting prospect that left many extremely footsore and exhausted. For three nights the party trudged through the hills, lying up in concealed positions by day lest they were spotted by Japanese aircraft or reconnaissance patrols. Leung's guerrillas faithfully guided them. As well as each man carrying a Lee-Enfield rifle or a pistol, in many cases both weapons, the group also hauled along six Bren light machine guns and a pair of Tommy guns. Just how effective the group would have been as infantrymen if they had run into serious Japanese opposition is debatable, as aside from Mike Kendall's SOE party and the Chinese guerrillas, the rest were sailors or civil servants.

Commander Gandy divided the men into 'watches', following shipboard practice. Each group was led by an SOE agent armed with a Tommy gun. A gang of Chinese coolies was hired to haul the sailors' kit bags and canned provisions. The Admiral, still missing his leg, was carried on a chair strapped between two long bamboo poles. The wounded civil servant MacDougall was also portaged in this manner, as he could no longer walk. Slow progress was made across broken and steep country, the march being conducted largely in silence. Several Japanese positions, already identified by Leung's guerrillas, were carefully skirted around, and the escape party was not detected. 'Three or four in our party were ill,' recalled Lieutenant Kennedy, 'one with dysentery and another suspected of having cholera. It was no wonder, when I think back on the food we had been eating.'

On day two of the hike, 27 December, the three groups set off at 8am. During a particularly steep climb up a mountain 26-year-old Lieutenant Tommy Parson, the former skipper of *MTB27* and Governor Sir Mark Young's naval aide-de-camp, developed heart trouble and collapsed. He also joined Chan and MacDougall in a bamboo-pole chair. The going was so bad, and, as some of the officers later admitted, the sailors so 'soft' after years of leisurely duties in Hong Kong, that the groups stopped for a ten-minute rest every hour.

Near the town of Danshui the escapees encountered a group of heavily armed and numerous Communist guerrillas, who blocked their path. If Chan and the British wanted to pass, the Communist leader announced that they would have to pay a 'fee' of 25,000 Chinese Nationalist Yuan. From his chair Admiral Chan engaged the Communists in a lively negotiation that took many hours to resolve, Chan initially only offering to pay 100 Yuan. After the kind of long-winded and loud haggling that the Chinese are famous for, Chan and the Communists eventually agreed upon the sum of 1,000 Nationalist Yuan. Major Goring later remarked that this figure equated in Pounds Sterling to only 2 shillings 6 pence per British escapee. 'That day we marched thirty-one miles and slept under a tree,' recalled Buddy Hide. 'It was winter time, and the coldest night we ever slept out in.'[10]

The 28 December was more of the same, with the group cross-country trekking through plains and over hills, occasionally passing through isolated villages where the locals would throng and gawk at the strange 'foreigners' as they passed through. But the day also brought the first signs of Free China when the weary column met advance elements of the Nationalist Army. The following day saw the escapees arrive at the first proper road they had seen since leaving Hong Kong. Japanese aircraft were spotted overhead on several occasions, but the column was not detected. The local Chinese military commander had bicycles sent down from Waichow so that the escapees could ride the final ten miles into the town. However, forty of the party were so foot-sore, exhausted or ill that they had to ride pillion. Protecting the town were some impressively huge water-filled anti-tank ditches, and the only way across was along single wooden planks that had been laid over the banks as rickety bridges. The Chinese bicycle drivers did not even hesitate, and with many a British serviceman clinging on for dear life, these plucky locals charged the planks and wobbled across to safety. Many of the British escapees said that crossing the anti-tank ditches was actually among the most frightening parts of their escape.

Waichow and sanctuary, however temporary, had finally been reached. The town was in ruins following a brief, but extremely brutal Japanese occupation. It was a major Nationalist supply port since Canton (now Guangzhou) had fallen to the Japanese. The Japanese had withdrawn from the town because they needed every available man for the assault on nearby Hong Kong, but Imperial forces had committed several bestial massacres including attempting to murder every Chinese man of military age that they encountered. Although the Japanese had left, their aircraft had continued to bomb the town regularly, as the Japanese were fully aware of the military importance of the position to the Chinese.

Waichow, its skyline dominated by a 1,000-year-old stone pagoda, was scarred and battered, many houses having been reduced to smouldering shells by Japanese bombs. Into these ruins had plunged a thousand refugees to swell the town's normal population, and a sizeable Chinese army under Lieutenant General Wong Da Fu, incongruously dressed in German army helmets and armed with Mauser rifles.

After a brief rest the British column was fallen in, and with the two youngest ratings carrying the White Ensign and the Chinese Nationalist Flag on either side of Admiral Chan and the local mayor, the column marched smartly through the Waichow town gates. They were greeted by the deafening cacophony of fire-crackers, as the Chinese celebrated the arrival of Chan and the British escapers, the streets thronged with laughing and smiling Chinese of all ages. The British party was housed in a former American missionary hospital in the centre of town and attended a lavish banquet that was hosted in their honour by General

Wong. On 30 December a group photograph was taken with the British party joined by some Chinese army officers. The British sang their National Anthem and afterwards local children presented each man with an orange, some cigarettes, a packet of biscuits, a tin of condensed milk and a small hand towel. Commander Gandy issued shore leave from 1–5pm, enabling the escapees to enter into some intense bargaining with local shopkeepers. In the meantime, MacDougall managed to telephone through a report of their miraculous escape to the British headquarters in Chongqing. Most of the group's small arms and ammunition were handed over to Leung's guerrillas, who would have more need of them, and preparations were begun for the very long journey back to British lines.

On 31 December the party marched down to the East River where they boarded two motor houseboats. Car engines that had been converted to run on charcoal gas powered these curious vessels. They broke down regularly. Each boat towed a long Chinese sampan made from a bamboo frame that was covered in rattan matting. Facilities were practically non-existent and the men were very cold as a freezing wind blew straight through the sampans, which were open at each end. The MTB crews enjoyed slightly better facilities aboard the motor houseboats while everyone else crowded aboard the sampans. Lieutenant Colonel F.G. Chauvin, Head of the British Military Mission China, had laid on the boats and sampans. Admiral Chan was escorted by a party of Nationalist soldiers to deter local river pirates and bandits from attacking the craft as they made their way to Lonquan. The three-man party from Z Force stayed behind in Waichow when the sailors left. They returned to where the MTBs had been scuttled and retrieved the heavy weapons that had been hidden by local villagers.

The journey down the river was slow, the boats often impeded by sandbars. Some of the men walked along the riverbanks during the daylight hours. Food was very limited – just a couple of bowls of boiled rice each day. A third motor houseboat was sent up from Waichow to relieve some of the overcrowding. The party then met up with the incongruously dressed Lieutenant Colonel Harry Owen-Hughes, the British liaison officer with the Chinese 7th Army. Dressed in a Chinese robe and hat, Owen-Hughes had been on the last plane out of Hong Kong and he was charged with organising the party's safe transit through southern China.

On arrival at Lonquan the MTB crews formed up and marched through the town, which celebrated the arrival of the British with a great show of fireworks, speeches and feasting. The Hong Kong escapees were now safely inside Chinese Nationalist territory, and although their journey back to their own lines would be long and fraught with many hazards and difficulties, they no longer feared being attacked by the Japanese. After battling weather, mountains and sickness the party reached Kunming and the start of the Burma Road. There they met not only the British Military Mission but also Mission 204, the British and Australian survivors of an attempt to supply and train local ethnic minorities in Burma to fight against the Japanese. Led by Major William Seymour, Mission 204 had only just managed to escape capture around Lashio in Burma and they had trekked for six weeks on foot to reach safety in Kunming.

The Royal Navy returned triumphant to Hong Kong in 1945, and a new naval base was constructed and named HMS *Tamar*. Many of the men who had escaped in December 1941 aboard the MTBs also returned to help rebuild the colony. Major Colin McEwan and Monia Talan were both awarded the MBE for their exceptional work with Z Force. McEwan later became Head of Physical Education in Hong Kong while Talan founded travel and laundry businesses. SOE's Mike Kendall ended the war a lieutenant colonel and was recommended for the George Medal, but his communist connections meant that he did not receive this high honour. David MacDougall, the civil servant who had swum for his life under heavy Japanese fire after the *Cornflower II* had been sunk, returned as Brigadier Colonial Secretary in 1945 and was briefly Governor in May–July 1947. Admiral Chan Chak became the first postwar mayor of Canton (now Guangzhou) while his subordinate and swimming companion in December 1941, Lieutenant Commander Henry Hsu finished his service as a vice admiral in the Chinese Nationalist Navy and was awarded an OBE by the British. He later moved to Taiwan after the Communist takeover.

As Britain slowly relinquished her Empire and her global military capability, the Navy's presence in the Far East became more and more focused on Hong Kong, until in 1997 the last British warship steamed out of the harbour and the colony was handed back to China. The former home of the Royal Navy in Hong Kong now serves as the main barracks for the People's Liberation Army garrisoning the new Special Administrative Region of China. By a final ironic twist the three British gunboats that the navy had evacuated deep into China as the Japanese pressed home their assaults on Hong Kong and Shanghai, HMS *Gannet*, *Falcon* and *Sandpiper*, were destined to have very long careers indeed. All three vessels were transferred to the Chinese Nationalist Navy in 1942, and their British crews brought out of China overland. HMS *Gannet* was the sister ship to the ill-fated *Peterel* and she was renamed *Ying Shan* (British Mountain) by the Chinese. Incredibly, this vessel patrolled the Yangtze River from 1949 as part of the Communist People's Navy until 1975. HMS *Falcon* went through several name changes, becoming the *Luan Huan* in 1942, then the *Ying The* (British Virtue) in 1948, and finally the *Nan Chiang* in 1950. She also continued patrolling the Yangtze until 1974. Finally, HMS *Sandpiper* was renamed *Ying Hao* (British Hero) in 1942 and did not retire from the People's Navy until 1974, all three vessels demonstrating their excellent design and suitability for the important work of keeping one of the world's major trade arteries safe. The era of the gunboat did not pass with the disappearance of the Royal Navy from the waterways and coast of China.

Chapter 3

The BAAG and a Great Escape

Eventually he was arrested and subjected to prolonged and severe torture by the Japanese who were determined to obtain information from him and to make him implicate the others who were working with him. Under this treatment he steadfastly refused to utter one word that could help the Japanese investigations or bring punishment to others. His fortitude under the most severe torture was such that it was commented upon by the Japanese prison guards. Unable to break his spirit the Japanese finally executed him.

George Cross citation for John Fraser, 25 October 1946

An army truck noisily reversed onto a beach, exhaust fumes rising in a cloud as the vehicle struggled through the soft sand. Two Japanese soldiers unhitched the tailgate, letting it swing down with a metallic crash. In the back of the truck three European men were pushed and prodded down onto the sand by more impatient Japanese guards. An officer stood casually to one side, smoking a cigarette and watching the three British officers with contempt. They were filthy, their hair matted with dirt and dried blood, faces unshaven, uniforms tattered and stained. Two of them were evidently sick; with the youngest carefully trying to help the other two hobble a few painful steps. Another command was bellowed in guttural Japanese and three shovels were thrown at the British officers' feet with a metallic crash, the Japanese in charge indicating with more shouting that they were each to dig their own graves. Summoning what dignity remained to them, Colonel Lan Newnham, Flight Lieutenant John Gray and Captain Douglas Ford wearily did what was demanded. For an hour the men dug in silence, their Japanese guards standing to one side smoking and talking in low voices until the terrible task was completed.

The officer in charge abruptly ordered each prisoner to stand in front of his hole while his men assembled themselves into a firing squad a few yards away. The prisoners muttered some final words to each other and perhaps shook hands before the word of command was bellowed, Arisaka rifles were levelled and the white men fell dead in a hail of bullets. The volley echoed across the beach and into the green hills beyond, a jarring epitaph for three of the bravest men the Japanese had held as prisoners, men who believed implicitly that their duty lay in continuing the fight against the enemy. Even though they had found themselves prisoners of a foe whose idea of warfare owed more to the Middle Ages than the era of international agreements and POW rights, these men had refused to submit.

The Japanese had made little preparation for prisoners of war when they had conquered Hong Kong in December 1941. This was partly deliberate, as the Japanese did not expect many of Hong Kong's defenders would surrender, believing that Major General Christopher Maltby's beleaguered garrison would instead perish in battle. In this belief, the Japanese again failed to understand Western military philosophy. The concept of fighting 'to the last man, and the last round' appealed deeply to the Japanese *bushido* code, which honoured death in battle as the most glorious expression of personal loyalty to God-Emperor Hirohito. Suicide was preferable to surrender; self-sacrifice in a *banzai* change was an honourable exit from the battlefield. British troops had fought to the death on many occasions during the nation's colonial campaigns, but normally only because they knew their enemies did not take prisoners. In the event 10,947 Allied troops became POWs after the fall of Hong Kong.

The Japanese plan involved moving the remnants of General Maltby's shattered Commonwealth battalions to hastily arranged camps located on Hong Kong Island and across Victoria Harbour in Kowloon. The two Indian Army battalions, the 5/7th Rajputs and 2/14th Punjabis, were ordered by the Japanese to assemble at the Botanical Gardens, located close to Murray Barracks in Central. Among them was a young officer who was to play a pivotal role in continued covert resistance to the Japanese. Captain Mateen Ahmed Ansari of the 5/7th Rajput Regiment came from a high-caste Indian family and was related to one of the rulers of a Princely State, a fact that was to bring him unwanted attention in due course from the *Kempeitai* Military Police.

On arrival at the Botanical Gardens the Japanese escort ordered Ansari and all of the other officers and sepoys to sit on the ground for several hours. Denied food or water, their guards did not hesitate to mercilessly beat the Indians with rifle butts if they had the temerity to raise any objections. Eventually the Japanese grew tired of this shambolic situation and they permitted small foraging parties to raid nearby British Army stores for food and other supplies. 'Garden ornamental birds rounded up and eaten,' recalled a British officer of one of the Botanical Gardens exhibits, 'Looted clothing from European homes and Murray Barracks stores.'[1]

British Army and Hong Kong Volunteer Defence Corps (HKVDC) prisoners were marched to a former barracks at Shamshuipo in Kowloon. Extensively damaged and then looted by locals during the battle for Hong Kong, the 'camp', located on Tonkin Street, was basically unfit for human habitation. Shamshuipo Barracks had been constructed for the British Army in the 1920s. The buildings on one side of the parade square were called Hankow Barracks, the opposite side Nanking Barracks. A large married quarters block called Jubilee Buildings was added later. The parade square that had once rung to the sounds of marching boots and the bellowed orders of sergeant majors was now littered with water-filled bomb and shell craters. Some of the buildings had caved-in roofs or were simply fire-blackened shells. After the fighting, desperate Chinese civilians had thoroughly looted the camp, even ripping out the doors, windows, window frames, electrical fittings and pipework.

The Japanese declared the camp open without giving any real thought to what the prisoners would eat, where they would wash and obtain clean drinking water, or any of the other basic amenities required to sustain life. Shamshuipo Camp would eventually become home to 5,777 POWs, many of them shipped over from Hong Kong. Lieutenant C.H. Fairclough of 5th Anti-Aircraft Regiment, Royal Artillery, was one British soldier who was sent to Shamshuipo. Like most POWs, his morale was at rock bottom as a ferry took him and his regiment across the narrow harbour to Kowloon. 'The ferry passed close to sunken ships and it was difficult to keep my heart from sinking with them. We then moved up Nathan Road to Shamshuipo; it was just a shuffle, an orderly shuffle.'[2]

Incredibly, although Shamshuipo was terrible, another newly designated POW camp was even worse. On the last day of December, eye-patch-wearing Brigadier Cedric Wallis marched with the remnants of East Brigade to a camp at North Point on Hong Kong Island. The Hong Kong Government had originally built North Point Camp as a refugee centre catering to Chinese escaping the horrific Japanese occupation over the border. It was used as a Japanese POW camp even before the Battle of Hong Kong was over when men of Brigadier John Lawson's Canadian West Brigade, captured in the beachhead battles, and the fighting at Jardine's Lookout and the Wong Nai Chong Gap on Hong Kong Island were moved in. Assigned primarily for the Canadians and Royal Navy prisoners, North Point was located on King's Road. With his one good eye, Wallis surveyed the 'camp', such as it was. A former Chinese refugee camp, North Point had been occupied by a Japanese mule company. Wallis and his companions were greeted by piles of mule dung both inside and outside of the accommodation huts, mountains of moldy straw, stinking puddles of animal urine as well as the dead bodies of soldiers who had perished during the recent fighting, many of which were in an advanced state of decomposition. The Japanese made it clear that this mess would be Wallis's duty to sort out. Two hundred prisoners were assigned to each pestilential and flyblown hut.

Brigadier Wallis was determined to look after his men, and after representations were made to the Japanese, he was permitted to organise a foraging party to leave the camp and obtain food, cooking utensils, medicine and even books. He managed to persuade the Japanese to let him have a British Army truck so that he could

45

drive to the island's hospitals and check on the wounded from his brigade, as well as move badly-needed supplies to the camp. At the same time, mutiny was brewing among the rank-and-file POWs, particularly among the raw Canadians, who felt badly let down by the British. In an echo of the kinds of 'soldiers' committees' formed during the Russian Revolution, 'during the first few days at North Point Camp a small number of Canadian Other Ranks started saying that now we were POWs, everyone was equal and that a camp committee should be chosen by them and that officers had nothing more to say,'[3] (wrote Wallis). 'Discipline had vanished,' recalled Private Wright of the Middlesex Regiment. 'We encountered our superiors only when it was unavoidable; they had lost the respect and authority conferred by rank and uniform.'[4] As well as directing their fury at senior officers, the prisoners also attacked one another. 'We scrounged, looted and stole, ignoring the respect we owed each other,' recalled Wright. 'We fought and argued over trivial matters and behaved like untutored and inexperienced children.'[5] The officers eventually managed, with the assistance of some of the remaining senior NCOs that the men still respected, to quell the revolutionary fervour. Wallis wrote that 'fortunately some measure of discipline was gradually re-established.'[6] A few months after the surrender the Royal Navy prisoners at North Point were moved to Shamshuipo. North Point then only held Canadians.

At Shamshuipo Camp in Kowloon things were equally difficult for General Maltby and his officers. Maltby recognised that it was of paramount importance to maintain discipline among the men, to remind the POWs that they were first and foremost soldiers and not simply a defeated rabble subject to the whims of a capricious and unpredictable enemy. He told his men that they must maintain their standards if they wished to survive the ordeal ahead, that they must try their best to hold sickness at bay by exercising personal cleanliness, and most importantly of all, they must respect their neighbours. After Maltby's lecture discipline began to be restored, but a wave of thieving committed by some of the lower ranks continued to be a problem for some months to come.

Gradual improvements at Shamshuipo were made by the prisoners themselves, and through the help of friends and local civilians still free outside of the wire. The Japanese held a morning roll call, or *tenko*, daily at 7am, during which the prisoners were expected to number off in Japanese. This could prove tricky to most squaddies unschooled in the intricacies of oriental languages, and sometimes roll call descended into a farce, with the infuriated Japanese getting progressively angrier every time they had to begin again. But aside from this daily ordeal, the prisoners were able to form a camp band that played regularly, and Europeans still at liberty in Hong Kong, along with some Chinese, managed to pass food and medicine through the wire to their friends among the prisoners. These little gifts helped enormously to stave off the worst of the Japanese starvation diet the prisoners were immediately subjected to and the medicine was especially well received, for the Japanese also withheld all medical supplies into the camps, which were very soon ravaged by a multitude of tropical diseases.

One man was determined to remain a captive at Shamshuipo for the briefest time possible. Unusual among potential escapees was both his age and his profession. 43-year-old Lieutenant Colonel Lindsay Ride was one of the most brilliant prisoners held by the Japanese in Hong Kong. Since 1928 he had been professor of physiology at the University of Hong Kong, investigating the blood groups of the peoples of the Pacific. 'Doc' Ride, as his students called him, had been born in Newsted, Victoria in 1898, the son of an Australian Presbyterian missionary. From a humble beginning, Ride had won a scholarship to the exclusive Scotch College, Melbourne before enlisting in the First World War. Wounded twice in combat in France, Ride had been invalided out of the army in 1919 and had decided to pursue a career in medicine at Melbourne University. In 1922 Ride had been a Rhodes Scholar to New College, Oxford, where, as 'Captain of Boats' he had earned the rowing moniker 'Blue' Ride. After working at Guy's Hospital in London, Ride had taken a professorship in Hong Kong. He had also taken a commission in the Hong Kong Volunteer Defence Corps, the colony's part-time militia, becoming commanding officer of its Field Ambulance Company. By 1938 Ride believed that war with Japan was imminent and presciently saw to it that his Canadian wife Mary and his sons, William and Edwin, were sent to Australia.

During the Battle of Hong Kong, Ride had taken command of the Combined Field Ambulance and had gone into captivity alongside his men. Always a resourceful man, Ride realised that he would be of more use outside of the wire, and with three trusted subordinates, this unlikely escapee broke out of Shamshuipo Camp on 9 January 1942. Ride's escape was only possible because of close cooperation between the imprisoned British, stay-behind Special Operations Executive agents and Chinese guerillas who were operating in Hong Kong's New Territories.

Ride travelled with two former university lecturers and fellow HKVDC officers, and a student named Francis Lee. During the final chaotic days before and after the fall of Hong Kong in December 1941, certain British troops had deliberately avoided capture and followed orders to create an escape network that would stretch from the colony into Free China. As we saw in Chapter 2, three SOE agents had escaped with Admiral Chan Chak's naval liaison party aboard the last serviceable Motor Torpedo Boats from Aberdeen Harbour. These agents ended up hidden on houseboats close to the town of Kukang in Xinhui County, Guangdong, on the Pearl River not far from Hong Kong and Macau.

Half a dozen British soldiers were camped out on more houseboats half a mile upriver from where Ride and the three-man SOE team were in hiding. This was the Special Duty Unit of the HKVDC, headed by Canadian Mike Kendall, also known as 'Z Force'. The unit's task was to stay behind in enemy-occupied territory and harass the Japanese. Long before the Japanese invasion of Hong Kong had begun, dumps of arms, supplies and medical stores were placed at three secret locations in the New Territories. Z Force's methods of harassment included sabotage, espionage, gathering military intelligence and blowing up bridges and other Japanese communications infrastructure. The men were armed with Thompson sub-machine guns and high explosives.

Lindsay Ride's small party eventually made their way south through Japanese territory into Free China, an incredible feat for a middle-aged professor, and one that earned him an OBE.

After his escape, Ride, a lieutenant colonel in the Indian Army, was authorised to create the British Army Aid Group (BAAG). Part of MI9, the shadowy wartime intelligence department that was responsible for assisting escapes from enemy POW camps, BAAG was headquartered in the pretty south Chinese city of Guilin in Guangxi Province, close to the border with French Indochina. Using a network of locally recruited agents, as well as Mike Kendall's Z Force, BAAG gathered intelligence on the Japanese and POWs across southern China and Hong Kong for Allied Command HQ in Chongqing.

Vital to BAAG's mission was Captain Colin McEwan, one of the SOE officers who had successfully escaped by MTB from Hong Kong in December 1941. McEwan was appointed BAAG station officer for Guangdong Province and relayed intelligence to and from the Hong Kong POW camps, and helped organise more escapes. 'By the winter of 1942 we had settled into a well organised unit and from our beginnings as an Escape and Evasion outfit, had developed into a fully fledged intelligence unit,'[7] wrote McEwan. Any men who were successfully smuggled out of Occupied China were retrained and fed back into the Allied war effort – for example, 128 escapees later joined Brigadier Orde Wingate's Chindit columns behind Japanese lines in Burma. Ride, the mastermind behind BAAG, earned the nickname 'The Smiling Tiger' to add to his other monikers, as well as a CBE in 1944. In total BAAG managed to get out 139 Allied POWs, 33 shot down American airmen, 314 British and Chinese military personnel who had managed to avoid capture in 1941, and 1,400 civilians.

None of these achievements were easy for Colonel Ride and BAAG. 'Ride's area was left to Ride, who had troubles enough with Chiang's officials, British bureaucrats, OSS [American equivalent to SOE] infiltration into his neighbourhood, and the Japanese, who often pressed him hard,'[8] writes SOE historian M.R.D. Foot. Such was the complex nature of undertaking any sort of operation with the Chinese that SOE's Far Eastern branch, Force 136, decided to allow old China hand Ride every discretion and in effect permitted him to operate his own little intelligence fief. The lack of interference from on high probably accounted for Ride's brilliant successes, and BAAG remained the only viable British military unit that was operational in China throughout the war, with most of the mainland relegated to the responsibility of the American OSS.

Some say Ride earned his CBE because of his influence over British policy in China. Ride realised that it was of vital import-ance for Britain to continue to exercise some influence over the course of the war in China. British prestige had been severely dented by the defeat at Hong Kong and the takeovers of the British concessions in Shanghai and Tientsin (now Tianjin). Ride knew that Japan would eventually be defeated, and that Britain would want to re-establish colonial control in Hong Kong – building bridges with the local resistance organisations was there-fore vital if such a plan was going to succeed. Without BAAG Britain could probably not have re-established its rule over Hong Kong when the Japanese surrendered, as moves were afoot during the war to give the territory back to China in return for more help from Chiang Kai-shek's Nationalists. Strong SOE representations to London prevented such a disastrous decision from being taken.

For the men that Ride had left behind in the camps in Hong Kong, life was grim, dangerous and often barbaric. Many witnessed Japanese atrocities first-hand, and many, including the most senior officers, had begun to consider ways to get their men out of Japanese captivity before they all died. The initially deplorable state of the POW camps had given way to food and medicine shortages, disease outbreaks and Japanese brutality.

Allied POWs regularly witnessed their Japanese guards abusing and murdering local Chinese civilians. Camp guards on duty in perimeter watchtowers often fired at Chinese families crossing Victoria Harbour in sampans in search for food. Each day some sentries left the camps and gathered up random Chinese civilians. The Chinese could be seen huddled together, crying out for mercy or impassive with resignation, their ankles bound together with chains. The Japanese would line them up beside the harbour, and then, emitting blood-curdling shrieks and cries, run the unfortunate Chinese through with their long bayonets. After they had been repeatedly stabbed the mutilated bodies were dumped into the harbour like refuse. Such was life for many Hong Kong Chinese under Japanese rule.

Maltreatment of captives was not limited to the Chinese beyond the wire. The Japanese authorities never lost an opportunity to humiliate British officers in front of their men, and break down their position of authority. In April 1942 at Shamshuipo Camp the Japanese decided to transfer most of the officers to a new camp, removing at a stroke the direct influence of officers on their men's behaviour, morale and welfare. The intention was to bring ordinary POWs completely under Japanese control and reduce them from being soldiers to mere coolies. One morning in April, 336 officers and 100 privates detailed to act as their batmen were paraded. Gathering what remained of their kit together, the officers and men were marched at bayonet point for six hours to Argyle Street Camp in Kowloon. Among the officers who were shipped off to Argyle Street were three who were to play a pivotal role in continuing resistance to the Japanese and in planning a Far Eastern 'Great Escape'. Lan Newnham was their leader.

Colonel Lanceray 'Lan' Newnham, aged 53, of the Middlesex Regiment was General Maltby's former Principal Operations Officer (GSO1) in the Fortress HQ battlebox during the defence of Hong Kong. Born in India in August 1889, his father was a lieutenant colonel and later British Military Attaché to the Tsar of Russia in St. Petersburg. Newnham attended Bedales School in Hampshire and excelled at tennis, playing on Centre Court at Wimbledon in 1914 shortly before the First World War broke out. During the war Newnham was wounded in action twice and awarded the Military Cross for bravery. After the war he had served in Egypt, the Rhineland and Bermuda, and was described by a contemporary as 'very reserved and conscientious, a strict teetotaller, non-smoker and a man who kept himself fit with golf and tennis under normal conditions. A first-class soldier, in fact.'[9] Newnham was determined to continue with an active military role even though he was a prisoner, and two younger officers of equal nerve and determination joined him in his covert activities.

Captain Douglas Ford had been born in Galashiels, Scotland in 1918, where his father was a factory manager. An excellent sportsman, he had been training to be an accountant when the war broke out in September 1939. Ford immediately joined the Royal Scots and was posted to the 2nd Battalion at Murray Barracks, Hong Kong. 'His school and his family imbued him with a sense of loyalty, compassion, independence of spirit and pride in traditional Scottish values,' wrote Douglas's brother Jim Ford of him. 'These self-same characteristics commanded respect from all those who knew him.'[10] Ford was held at Shamshuipo Camp where he had managed to make contact with BAAG agents. Newnham was moved to the officer's camp at Argyle Street.

The other young officer who worked closely with Newnham and Ford was 31-year-old Flight Lieutenant Hector Gray of the RAF. Known as 'Dolly' to his comrades, and in contrast to the public-school Newnham and Ford, Gray came from a large working-class family in Kent. He had joined the RAF in January 1927 at the age of fifteen as an apprentice at RAF Halton in Buckinghamshire. He qualified as a wireless operator mechanic and served with the Fleet Air Arm. By 1936 he was a flight sergeant, and had served with 48 and 148 Squadrons as well as the experimental Long Range Development Unit. His greatest claim to fame before his brave exploits in Hong Kong was as the wireless operator on the RAF's successful world record attempt for longest non-stop flight – 7,158 nautical miles from Ismailia, Egypt to Darwin, Australia, with two Wellesley aircraft, completed over forty-eight hours in November 1948. This feat had earned Gray the Air Force Medal. At Shamshuipo and Argyle Street Camps, Gray arranged for medical supplies to be smuggled into the camps. He also ran a clandestine news service to circulate news from outside the camps to the POWs.[11]

Argyle Street Camp, on the corner of Argyle Street and Lomond Road, was in a condition almost identical to that of Shamshuipo when the first officer prisoners had marched in. Its original purpose had been to house Chinese Nationalist soldiers who had crossed the border into the colony in 1938 seeking sanctuary from the Japanese. Immediately after the British surrender the camp had housed Indian prisoners, many of whom were riddled with disease, until they were moved out to nearby Mau Tan Chung Camp to make way for the British officers. Between the departure of the Indians and the arrival of the British, locals had, in common with all of the Hong Kong camps, systematically looted the place almost bare. Enclosed by a tall electric fence and six guard towers, the camp was initially completely devoid of food. Among the senior officers transferred was Brigadier Cedric Wallis, who had just been released from Bowen Road Military Hospital after a bout of sickness. General Maltby was also transferred, and he fell into an understandable depression. Maltby was 'a very distressed and disillusioned man. It took me several months sharing the same room to cheer him up and convince him that, far from our troops not being deserving of honours, as he believed, there often is far greater gallantry in defence than in attack,'[12] wrote Wallis. 'I eventually got him to see that he was being unfair to many brave men.'[13]

Very close to Argyle Street was Ma Tau Chung Camp, located on the road of the same name. This camp held men from the two Indian battalions that the Japanese had captured. Among them were a dozen extremely brave and resourceful Indian officers who were to prove themselves vital to the POW intelligence gathering and escape network in Hong Kong. The 500–600 Indian POWs who had steadfastly refused to join the Japanese-led Indian National Army were held in very bad conditions at Ma Tau Chung Camp, and a great many died.

Some of the imprisoned civilians were also to play a vital role in the POW covert organisation. British and Allied civilians, along with some of the older or lamer members of the HKVDC, were held at Stanley Road Camp, a location that was also used as an interrogation centre and prison by the *Kempeitai*. Assistant Attorney General John Fraser, a senior colonial civil servant under Governor Sir Mark Young (who was held separately at Woosung Camp, Shanghai) became a secret member of BAAG and was intimately involved in the plotting. Fraser had been awarded the Military Cross twice during the First World War, so bravery was not something in short supply in the middle-aged administrator.

Contact was established between the POWs at Argyle Street and BAAG operatives via the regular wood deliveries that arrived by truck at the camp. The Chinese driver, who was a BAAG courier, would give a warning cough and then drop a cigarette packet unobtrusively onto the ground when the Japanese guard was not looking. Lieutenant Harris of the Royal Engineers 'picked it up and a scrap of paper inside, when held up to a piece of smoldering charcoal, revealed a message. Shipping and military information were passed back when a [British] captain from the Punjab regiment, who spoke Hindustani and occasionally worked in a vegetable garden next to the Indian POW camp, was able to tap into the Indian intelligence network. Medicine and other items such as compasses were smuggled into Argyle Street.'[14]

Colonel Isao Tokunaga, nicknamed 'Fat Pig' by the POWs, was in overall charge of the Hong Kong prison camps. He was a violent and unscrupulous officer who the prisoners fortunately saw little of, as he preferred living in Kowloon with his Chinese mistress. As with all Japanese prison camps, English-speaking interpreters were provided by the army. Though civilians, these men, most of whom had lived in English-speaking countries before the war, were permitted to wear officer's uniforms minus rank badges and carried weapons. Many abused their positions mercilessly. The POWs gave them various secret nicknames based upon their appearances and demeanors. The POWs knew Genichiro Nimori as 'Panama Pete' – he was a small Japanese-American from Chicago whom Tokunaga appointed chief interpreter for the Hong Kong area.[15] 'Slap Happy' was the nickname of Kanao Inouye, a violent Japanese-Canadian who enjoyed hitting prisoners in the face while talking to them. He was also derisively called 'Shat in Pants' because his uniform was so badly tailored that the seat of his trousers formed a pendulous bag that hung down to his knees.

Many of the camp guards were not Japanese but Indians. Numbering around 400 in total, the Indians were mostly local civilians and former members of the Hong Kong Police. Most were hard on the white prisoners, and this was encouraged by the Japanese, as was the humiliation of British officers.

But a special hatred was reserved for the conscripted Korean guards, and their cruelty towards Allied POWs soon became legendary throughout the Japanese prison camp system. The Japanese looked down upon the Koreans, Korea having been a Japanese colony since just before the First World War, and they humiliated them at every opportunity. 'Japanese guards treated Koreans no better than prisoners,' writes Gavan Daws in *Prisoners of the Japanese*, 'like another breed of mongrel dog to kick ... One said to an Englishman, *Inggeris-korean samo* [English-Korean same], *all prisoner nippon*. Another said it to an Australian: *You me samo*. But for every one miserable Korean who saw life in the camps that way, there were all the others, Hatchet Face, Shadrach the Shitbag, and the rest, taking out their rage against the Japanese on the prisoners.' As Daws writes, 'Samo? said the Australian, with feeling. Like hell'.[16] The only relief for the Koreans was to take out their frustrations on the prisoners, which they did with alacrity. Prisoners were the only life-form lower on the Japanese military scale of value after the press-ganged Korean guards.

Aside from physical abuse, the Japanese found new ways to torture their prisoners *en masse*. One method was withholding medicines on the orders of Japanese medical officers. The camps were overcrowded, as Lan Newnham noted of Argyle Street: 'We now have 550 all ranks in Camp measuring 180×140 [feet].'[17] Tropical diseases soon tore through the POWs, greatly exacerbated by starvation and the deliberate withholding of drugs by Colonel Tokunaga's chief medical officer, Dr Shunkichi Saito. The Canadians got the worst of it because there had not been time to inoculate them against diphtheria before they arrived in Hong Kong before the battle. Between June 1942 and February 1943 at Shamshuipo Camp, 714 cases of diphtheria were recorded, resulting in 112 deaths caused directly by Saito's medical negligence.

Some of the overcrowding was relieved when 1,816 British and Commonwealth POWs were taken from their camps and marched down to the docks and loaded aboard the *Lisbon Maru* for the journey to Japan. Most never made it, drowning at sea after their unmarked transport ship was torpedoed and sunk by an American submarine.

If their comrades back in the Hong Kong camps thought that the Japanese would keep them alive the indications were not good. On 1 November 1942 the Japanese unexpectedly issued Red Cross parcels. The Japanese had looted the parcels of anything that took their fancy, but there was enough left, particularly of food items the Japanese found unpalatable, to raise the prisoners' morale greatly. A prisoner wrote: 'Bully beef, cigarettes, jam, meat and vegetable rations, cocoa, dried fruit, sugar and clothing ... We now had reason to hope that these shipments might be repeated and that we stood a good chance of surviving.'[18] He was wrong, however, and this proved to be the only occasion during the war that the Japanese released Red Cross parcels to their intended recipients. Staying put in Hong Kong was looking like an increasingly bleak prospect for Allied POWs. If disease didn't get you, starvation probably would in the long term, not to mention the uncertainty of being shipped off to some unknown destination as a slave labourer.

In January 1942 the Japanese emptied Argyle Street and moved the prisoners to Shamshuipo, North Point and Ma Tau Chung Camps. After a number of successful escapes from Shamshuipo, Argyle Street was re-opened by the Japanese in mid-1942 as an officer's camp.

The decision to stage a Far Eastern 'Great Escape' similar to that successfully made by RAF prisoners held by the Germans at Stalag Luft III on 25 March 1944, when seventy-six men managed to break out of the camp using escape tunnels, was perfectly sensible. Of all the places where Allied soldiers were imprisoned, Hong Kong was the geographically closest to friendly forces. Colonel Ride's BAAG had managed to establish direct contact between Free China and the camps. In between these two locations were a network of BAAG agents and informers, as well as the SOE's Z Force and friendly Chinese guerrillas. BAAG had successfully smuggled out small groups of POWs from the camps to freedom on many occasions. The chances of a mass breakout succeeding certainly had a greater chance in Hong Kong than anywhere else in the Occupied Territories. But would it be worth the cost in human lives if the plan went wrong?

The British managed to suborn some of their Indian guards into helping them and informing on the Japanese. It was one thing to have direct links with BAAG, but communication between the different prison camps in Hong Kong was considerably more difficult to establish. Indian soldiers were the key. With the assistance of ten extremely brave Indian Army officers, the British managed to establish an intelligence network between the dispersed POW camps. The Japanese were not only employing Indians to guard the prisoners, but also were using Indians as coolies all over Hong Kong at many sensitive military establishments. They cleaned up, worked in kitchens and stores, cleared up war damage and drove vehicles. The Indians were persuaded to pass on information concerning Japanese troop dispositions, numbers and types of ships in the harbour and anything else considered useful. The British POW network then passed this intelligence on to BAAG. Several British and Canadian officers even escaped from their camps for short periods to carry out espionage missions before returning secretly to captivity. Such was their dedication to the war effort that these officers never considered staying free and making use of the BAAG escape routes to freedom.

One Indian officer who was intricately involved in the POW intelligence network was an early target for the Japanese. Captain Mateen Ansari of 5/7th Rajputs was hauled off to Stanley Prison when the Japanese realised that he was related to Indian royalty. The *Kempeitai* demanded that Ansari renounce his allegiance to the British and help them to foment discontent among Indian POWs. His flat refusal led to his being starved and brutalised until May 1942 when the Japanese gave up and returned the young officer to his camp. Ansari immediately resumed his covert work for the POW intelligence network, even though he had a large metaphorical target painted on his back.

The driving force behind the POW intelligence network was Colonel Newnham. But Newnham decided to go further than just providing intelligence to BAAG. He conceived of an idea to launch a mass escape before the Japanese reduced the men's health to such an extent that they would be physically unable to make a break for freedom.

The plan was, that with the aid of the network of informers that Newnham and his conspirators had already put in place, and with the aid of local Chinese guerrillas, a large cache of arms, ammunition and food would be secreted in the nearby hills of the New Territories. A diversionary raid would be made by a force of guerrillas against one of the camps, possibly accompanied by an Allied air raid from China, so as to throw the Japanese into confusion. Under the cover of these twin attacks there would be simultaneous breakouts from the three camps at Shamshuipo, North Point and Argyle Street.

The risks that Newnham's plan entailed were formidable. The POWs would have to take on armed Japanese, Korean and Indian guards who were generally well fed and in the prime of life, and also deal with attacks from the local Japanese garrison, whose reaction to any mass breakout would be to shoot on sight all escapees. The death toll among the POWs in the operation was expected to be around 30 per cent. 'In all three camps the general standard of health had reached a very low level,' wrote General Maltby, who harboured grave reservations about Newnham's plan when his subordinate laid it before him. 'Any escape would have caused severe and immediate repercussions and further privations that would have been fatal to many,' he wrote. The Japanese would have murdered every POW that they laid their hands on. They already executed most men who tried to escape as a matter of policy, but if the escapees had killed or injured Japanese soldiers during the attempt, the Japanese would have had no qualms in committing wholesale massacre. The chances of the Japanese also committing further acts of revenge against the local population, as well as at other POW centres throughout Asia, were great. Such an attempt could also have immediately destroyed the BAAG intelligence network, depriving the Allies of valuable military information concerning what was going on inside occupied Hong Kong. But these risks had to be weighed against the slow deterioration of the POWs. Was it better to risk everything, or sit tight and watch thousands die slowly from disease and malnutrition? For a man like Maltby, who cared deeply about the lives of his soldiers, Newnham's plan led to a great deal of soul-searching and considered thought.

General Maltby's final assessment of the breakout plan made for worrying reading. Such was the level of malnutrition and disease throughout the three camps that fully 'one-third of our numbers, owing to their physical state, would have had to be abandoned,' wrote Maltby. Taking on well-armed and motivated Japanese troops with only rifles and side arms would have led to high casualties among the POWs, and for many the breakout would have been tantamount to a suicide mission. 'Another third we reckon would probably have fallen in the subsequent fighting,' was Maltby's terse assessment. 'The remainder, we hoped, would be able to make their way to freedom and so continue to parti-cipate in the war.'[19] Could any commander condemn one-third of his men to almost certain death, probably two thirds judging by the vindictive nature of their Japanese overlords? Could Maltby have this on his conscience?

Perhaps if General Maltby had known what the Japanese were going to do to his men over the long years of imprisonment, he

might have authorised the escape plan in the expectation that it would *save* lives.

For example, the Japanese were to ship thousands of POWs out of Hong Kong to Japan as slave labourers. The second large draft shipped out consisted of 1,800 British POWs aboard the afore-mentioned transport ship *Lisbon Maru*. The Japanese did not mark POW transport ships in direct violation of international agree-ments and this policy resulted in over 10,000 Allied prisoners being killed in horrific 'friendly fire' incidents as the American, British and Dutch navies targeted Japanese merchant ships through a massively effective submarine campaign. A single torpedo fired from the USS *Grouper* on 1 October 1942 off the Zhoushan Archipeligo near Shanghai struck the *Lisbon Maru*. Of the 1,800 POWs aboard only 748 ever saw Britain again. Hundreds more who were shipped out of Hong Kong aboard other ships died in mines and factories in Japan and elsewhere. The Canadians paid a horrific price for their capture. During the Battle of Hong Kong 290 Canadians were killed in action. But a further 264 died in captivity, mainly from disease. Out of a total 1,050 Canadian soldiers who had been sent to Hong Kong, 554 remain buried there today.

After very careful consideration Christopher Maltby reluctantly overruled Newnham and did not give his permission for the 'Great Escape' to proceed. In any analysis of the plan it is tempting to follow Maltby's mindset and think that he was saving Allied lives by preventing a potentially disastrous mass escape. We have the benefit of hindsight, whereas Maltby could not know that a third of his men would be dead anyway by the end of the war from starvation, disease, brutality and overwork, and other causes. His humanity and concern for the lives of his soldiers overrode his commitment to such a risky and perhaps even foolhardy venture. Neither could he have predicted his own cruel treatment in Manchuria by the Japanese later in the war. Newnham's plan remains one of the great 'what ifs' of the Second World War.

While Newnham and his confederates were planning a mass breakout from their camp, Colonel Ride at BAAG was busily trying to organise a similar scheme for the civilian internees imprisoned

at Stanley. The internment camp's population consisted of women and children, older men and white Hong Kong Police officers. In July 1942 Ride made contact by letter with Duncan Sloss at Stanley Camp, his former colleague and Vice-Chancellor of the University of Hong Kong. 'My dear Sloss, this is an attempt to set up a regular news service between us,' wrote Ride, asking Sloss to provide him with an up-to-date list of the internees by nationality, and 'also a report on the treatment, condition and casualties in the camp. I am trying to arrange the 'escape' to liberation of all children; if this plan ever gets as far as the camp, please do all you can to persuade mothers to let their children go ...' It was one thing to encourage and assist in the escape of military POWs – after all, it was the duty of captured soldiers to attempt to escape. But the escape of civilian non-combatants was an entirely different and much riskier proposition.

Several individuals and small groups of civilians had managed to slip out of Stanley to freedom, but the risks to life and limb were considerable. 'Once the decision to escape had been taken, which was not to be done lightly in view of the consequences of being caught, or the likely reprisals on the other internees, the problems to be tackled were daunting,' wrote Hong Kong police-man George Wright-Nooth, who was an internee at Stanley, 'the most obvious being the wide stretch of water between the island and the mainland.'[20] Ride's final plan for a Stanley break-out hoped to bridge the water by positioning a motor-powered Chinese junk 500 yards off Stanley Point. The plan was for fifty internees including women and children, with the assistance of Chinese guerrillas, to swim to the boat. Perhaps fortunately for all concerned, this rather hare-brained scheme was shelved when a suitably powered junk could not be found.

Real success for BAAG would continue to lie with the imprisoned soldiers, sailors and airmen in the military camps. Unfortunately, for some time the *Kempeitai* had been suspicious that the British were operating some kind of covert operation within the Hong Kong camps, and that this probably also involved some outside help. In mid-June 1943 the Japanese military police swooped down and managed to break up the POW intelligence network with disastrous consequences for those involved. In a wave of arrests Colonel Newnham and many of his officers and men were taken

a man such as Suga was a rare personality indeed. Although Suga's beliefs appeared to run contrary to commonly held stereo-types of the brutal and sadistic Japanese camp commandant, many of his subordinates were unfortunately psychotic lunatics and raving nationalists who inflicted appalling suffering upon their prisoners.

Suga was based at the joint POW/civilian internment centre at Batu Lintang, far away from the main concentration of Allied POWs at Sandakan. His physical distance from the three camps at Sandakan probably meant that he could exercise very little control over his subordinate officers. In command at Sandakan was Captain Susumi Hoshijima, an officer with a distinct penchant for brutality, sadism and irrationality in equally disturbing measure.

Captain Hoshijima's greatest nemesis was about to arrive at Sandakan. Lionel Matthews was a 29-year-old decorated captain in the Australian Army Signal Corps from Norwood, a suburb of Adelaide. Matthews would prove to be a considerable thorn in the side of the Japanese, and a man for whom the words 'never surrender' could have been his motto. Matthews had first arrived in Singapore on Valentines Day 1941 as part of the Major General H. Gordon Bennett's much vaunted 8th Australian Division. The brown-haired, blue-eyed former department store salesman who sported a neatly trimmed moustache quickly impressed his superiors during the Battle of Gemas, one of the bloody engage-ments fought by the Australians during the retreat down the Malayan Peninsula. Then Lieutenant Matthews went out under heavy Japanese artillery and mortar fire to restore communica-tions between his brigade headquarters and its subordinate units. 'He climbed a pole and held together wires to get the central message through, he did it several times a day,' recalled his son David. 'The Japanese would be sniping at him, aiming at him with machine-gun fire but they still didn't get him.'[1] He also 'succeeded in laying cable over ground strongly patrolled by the enemy and thus restoring communication between his Divisional HQ and the HQ of a Brigade at a critical period.'[2] Awarded the Military Cross, Matthews was promoted to captain in January 1942. Captured when General Percival surrendered Singapore in February 1942, Matthews was initially imprisoned at the infamous Changi Camp, the vast holding centre for Percival's shattered and demoralised

Malaya Command. Back in Australia his wife Lorna and young sons heard little of his activities, or his ultimate fate, until 1945.

On 8 July 1942 the first large movement of prisoners to Borneo was made when 'Force B' was shipped out of Changi Camp by the Japanese authorities. It consisted of 1,500 fit and healthy Australians under the command of Lieutenant Colonel Walsh of the 2/10th Field Regiment, Royal Australian Artillery. They were sent by ship to Sandakan in the colony of British North Borneo. Lieutenant Rod Wells recalled his first sight of Sandakan from the transport ship: 'From the sea it's lovely. With the red chalk hills on the side of Berhala Island it really is impressive. I suppose for a split moment we thought, with a sigh of relief, that here's some beautiful, peaceful land where there may not be any Japanese.'[3] Wells and his comrades were soon disabused of such notions once they had landed.

Captain Hoshijima had overseen the building of three camps at Sandakan. When they arrived 'Force B' was imprisoned inside Camp 1. They had been brought to Borneo to complete a specific task – to help Japanese engineers construct two airstrips, aircraft dispersal areas, and a system of supply roads through the thick jungle. The work was difficult, and the Japanese were hard task-masters. The typical working day began at 7.30am and continued through to 5.30pm in an enervating heat. Initially, the prisoners were properly fed and the guards largely refrained from physically abusing them. 'We had it easy the first twelve months ... we used to get flogged, but we had plenty of food and cigarettes,' recalled Private Keith Botterill of the 2/19th Australian Infantry Battalion. 'We actually had a canteen in the prison camp ... It was a good camp.'[4] The fact that only six prisoners died during their first year at Sandakan testifies to the 'hands off' approach of the Japanese.

Just after their arrival from Singapore, eleven members of 'Force B' managed to slip away from Sandakan, but they did not manage to remain free for long. Splitting up into two parties, one group of six men took refuge deep in the jungle in an abandoned timber cutter's hut. Officers at the camp had provided the groups with what they could spare in the way of an escape kit – some tinned rations, anti-malarial medicines and a compass, but few rated their chances. They were thousands of miles behind Japanese lines, and their white faces would stick out like sore thumbs among the native population, which was itself of unknown loyalty. They also faced a compendium of horrible tropical diseases that festered in the jungle and soon weakened even the healthiest Allied prisoners.

The group in the jungle eventually began to run short of food and they were forced to risk recapture by going to a Chinese farmer's house and asking for help. Fortunately for them the farmer, Chu Li Tsia, was no friend of the Japanese, and he directed the desperate escapees to the home of a Mr Phillips, a member of the local resistance and the manager of the North Borneo Timber Company. Four Australians turned up on his doorstep. Phillips knew that getting these malnourished and ill Australians out of Borneo and to Allied lines was an almost impossible undertaking, and hiding them risked the chance of discovery by the Japanese and the compromising of a carefully built-up clandestine resistance organisation. Phillips, faced with a terrible decision, felt that he had no choice but to turn in the escapees to the Japanese to save the lives of his network. A local villager who probably similarly feared awful reprisals against his people if Allied prisoners were discovered hiding in his village turned in the other two sick Australians. The *Kempeitai* Military Police quickly collected the prisoners and sent them all to Sandakan Jail.[5]

The other group of five Australians fared a little better, managing to remain on the run for an astounding five months, which was no mean feat considering the terrible hazards that they faced. Another Chinese local named Foo Seng Chow had caught them stealing vegetables from his garden and he put them in touch with the resistance, who fed them and also secured for them a small boat. The POWs intended to sail the boat all the way back to Australia. Unfortunately, the season and the tides were against them and the boat ended up stuck on a mud bank close to shore shortly after they launched themselves on their daring voyage. Fearing discovery by Japanese patrols, the Australians swam back to land but they were observed by local villagers, some of whom were not friendly. The *Kempeitai* offered cash rewards to those locals who turned in Allied escapers alive and for extremely poor natives it was tempting to cooperate with their new masters. The Australians, all of them sick with beriberi and malaria, were sent for trial at the Bornean capital Kuching. Fortunate not to be sentenced to death, the men were given prison sentences and transported to the notoriously harsh Outram Road Jail in Singapore to serve out their punishments.[6]

The Japanese soon required more labourers. POWs were shipped in from Changi and elsewhere and housed inside the two empty camps at Sandakan. In April 1943 a group of 776 British prisoners arrived at Camp 2 in two parties from Jesselton (now Kota Kinabalu), the largest settlement in Sabah province. Compared to the Australians, the British prisoners were in poor physical condition after a long and convoluted journey from Changi. The fittest 206 British prisoners arrived on 8 April, with the rest, totalling 570, arriving in camp on the 18th. Out of the second party 240 men were very sick with malnutrition and tropical diseases. Captain Hoshijima expressed no particular interest in their predicament and ordered them to be crowded into wooden huts, seventy-four men to each building.

At the same time that the British arrived at Sandakan a group of Formosan Chinese guards from Taiwan arrived, brutal little men who despised the Japanese almost as much as they hated the POWs. Taiwan was a Japanese colony and the locals had been forced to adopt Japanese names and speak the Japanese language. The Japanese treated the Formosan soldiers as their inferiors. The humiliation and impotent fury felt by the Formosans towards their overlords found expression in their appalling treatment of the only people lower than themselves – the prisoners in their charge. The new Formosan guards took to delivering mass beatings of POW work details under the flimsiest of pretexts. 'My gang would be working all right and then would be suddenly told to stop ... The men would then be stood with their arms outstretched horizontally, shoulder high, facing the sun without hats,' recalled Warrant Officer Class 1 Hector 'Bill' Sticpewich of the Royal Australian Army Service Corps. The guards would form themselves into two groups, one group covering the prisoners with their rifles 'and the others doing the actual beating. They would walk along the back of us and ... smack us underneath the arms, across the ribs and on the back,' said Sticpewich. 'They would give each man a couple of bashes ... if they whimpered or flinched they would get a little more.'[7]

Hoshijima also delighted in introducing mediaeval tortures as 'punishment' for small transgressions of his rules. The commandant ordered the construction of a special place of torture to punish offenders known to the prisoners as 'The Cage'. It was placed next to a large tree in Camp 1 and was a wooden structure 130cm high and 170cm long with iron bars on all sides. Prisoners were forced to sit at attention inside the cage all day long and no bedding or mosquito netting was provided. Private Keith Botterill experienced this horror first hand:

> The time I was in for forty days there were seventeen of us in there. No water for first three days. On the third night they'd force you to drink till you were sick. For the first seven days you got no food. On the seventh day they started feeding you half camp rations ... Every evening we would get a bashing, which they used to call physical exercise ...[8]

The last camp at Sandakan, Camp 3, was finally filled in June 1943 when a fresh group of POWs was shipped in. Known as 'Force E', it consisted of 500 Australians direct from Changi.

Lionel Matthews did not view his circumstances as a reason to stop fighting the Japanese. Within a harsh and terrifying environment Matthews began to create an organisation that would eventually pose a serious threat. Captain Hoshijima strictly forbade any communication between the three camps, and anyone who disobeyed this order was severely punished. Matthews's first task was to break Hoshijima's prohibition on inter-camp communication by the setting up of a secret network. He also began to address the central problems that were faced by the POWs, namely a lack of medicines to treat the various tropical diseases that stalked them more efficiently than their guards, as well as a shortage of food. Matthews's efforts in smuggling food into the camps through his contacts with locals went some way to alleviating the chronic malnutrition. Matthews could only do this by building contacts with the world beyond the perimeter fence, a decidedly dangerous undertaking as he never knew for sure who could be trusted and who could have turned them over to the Japanese in return for cash.

The Japanese allowed Matthews to command a small group of prisoners who were permitted outside unsupervised by guards to collect nuts. A grove of palm-oil trees behind the local police station became Matthews's connection point to the local underground resistance movement. The police put Matthews in touch with local British doctor Jim Taylor, one of several doctors and dentists that the Japanese had not interned because their skills were desperately needed. Although under close watch, Dr Taylor risked his life smuggling medicines to the camps, along with another civilian, Mrs Lillian Funk. This intrepid lady had wisely converted some of her assets to gold, pearl, foreign currency and gemstones just before the Japanese had captured Sandakan, and she had sewn these valuables into the hems of her clothes. She sold what she needed to purchase food and medicines for the POWs. These supplies 'not only kept up the morale and courage of the prisoners but undoubtedly saved the lives of many.'[9]

Matthews organised a group of twenty trusted officers and NCOs at the camp into an *ad hoc* intelligence-gathering group. Using sympathetic local intermediaries among the indigenous population, Matthews's group made contact with British civilians being held in an internment camp on nearby Bahara Island. Natives often entered the camps to perform various menial chores, and British and Australian working parties outside the camps also had contact with locals. Matthews was playing an extremely dangerous game, for all it took was one informer and his entire organisation would be blown to the Japanese, with terminal consequences for all those involved.

At the civilian camp on Bahara Island was Charles Smith, the former Governor of North British Borneo. Smith immediately realised the value of Captain Matthews's intelligence work and he appointed him to the command of the North British Armed Constabulary, a native police force that remained in operation under Japanese control. Many of its officers and men remained secretly loyal to the British. 'In great danger he organised that body in readiness for a rising against the Japanese and also organised a movement amongst the loyal native population of Sandakan for a similar purpose.'[10] Many locals were of Chinese descent, and their treatment by the Japanese was harsh and discriminatory, engendering great hatred. Many were happy to help the British war effort if it meant an end to the Japanese occupation.

With the help of friendly locals and the civilian internees, Matthews built up a dossier of intelligence concerning the organisation and deployment of Japanese forces in North Borneo, their strengths and bases, supply situation and details about the local geography. Matthews intended to pass all of this valuable information on to the Allies in the hope that it would assist them in eventually liberating Borneo.

The gathering and caching of firearms was another of Matthews's efforts, the intention eventually being to launch an insurrection against the Japanese, most probably timed to coincide with an Allied invasion of the island. Matthews's group needed information about the progress of the war, so using their network they managed to smuggle radio parts into their camp and constructed a simple wireless receiver. It was a mission fraught with danger, but two Australian officers, Lieutenant Rod Wells and Lieutenant Gordon Weynton of the Australian Signal Corps, put together the crystal detector, valves and headphones.

The job of getting a signal on the basic wireless took weeks of effort, but one day through the crackling static came a familiar English public school voice that confidently announced: 'This is the BBC'. It was the voice of freedom. Barely able to contain their excitement, Matthews ordered the delicate set wrapped in a water-proof groundsheet and carefully hidden inside an unused latrine pit.[11] A system of nocturnal radio monitoring was set up, whereby news was carefully written down by the listeners and then distributed to the POW officers, who in turn passed it on verbally to their men. Morale was raised considerably.

Captain Matthews knew that it was important to demonstrate to the locals that the war was turning against the Japanese, so as to secure their continued support for his secret activities. Russ Ewin was tasked with passing the latest bulletins to the resistance, one of the contact points being the local Constabulary station. 'The police station was the contact for me. I would report each day to Lionel [Matthews]. If he had anything to be taken out of the camp, I would take it,' recalled Ewin. The risk of being caught on one of these missions did not bear thinking about. Ewin would most probably have been horribly tortured by the *Kempeitai* and then shot if caught red-handed with such inflammatory material. 'It usually was the news,' said Ewin of the packages that Lionel gave him, 'and it was rolled up tightly in a wad of paper sealed with sealing wax. When we came to the police station, I would just nod my head slightly, and the police sergeant, Sergeant Abin, who I had met, would just watch my hand and I would open it and drop the news. He would pick it up afterwards ...'[12]

This operation went smoothly, but the news of the progress of the war that he heard from the BBC emboldened Matthews to pursue another plan that unfortunately proved to be his undoing. Any uprising that was going to be made by the remaining fit prisoners, the members of the Constabulary and other sympathisers needed to be carefully timed. Matthews knew the prisoners needed a radio transmitter so they could communicate directly with the Allies, as their current wireless set could only receive signals. The process of smuggling the parts into the camp appeared to go smoothly, but the weakness of Matthews's organisation was the large number of people involved outside of the wire. Unfortunately, one of the Chinese sympathisers involved in procuring the radio parts, Joe Ming, was betrayed to the *Kempeitai* by a disgruntled contact during the course of black market negotiations at one of the local airstrips. The *Kempeitai* moved with their customary swiftness to try and discover the extent of the resistance organisation and brutally tortured Ming and his family until they broke and started naming names.

For Matthews and some of his men the game was up. He had long known the terrible risks that he was running, but his sense of duty had outweighed any concerns that he may have had for his own personal safety or survival. 'He was in a position where he could have escaped on numerous occasions by means of help of an organisation set up by the Chinese but he declined, electing to remain where his efforts could alleviate the sufferings of his fellow prisoners.'[13]

The Allied conspirators who had been named by Joe Ming, including some local men, were removed to *Kempeitai* headquarters in Kuching. For three long and terrible months Matthews and his friends were horribly tortured. They endured vicious beatings and the infamous 'water treatment' where a hose was placed inside the victim's mouth and water pumped in until the victim lost consciousness. They were hung by the arms for long periods and had their fingernails pulled off with pliers. One of their number, Johnny Funk, whose wife Lillian had sold gold and pearls to buy medicine for the prisoners, recalled the treatment that he received from the Japanese: 'They had four bungalows which were used for torture rooms. One form of torture was to make you kneel on a plank specially carved like spikes. They then placed a heavy plank behind the knees and two Japanese got on each end and worked it like a see-saw.' The *Kempeitai* was inventive in the methods it employed. 'Another torture was carried out by a Jujitsu expert. He flung you all around the room. He badly twisted limbs and used his boots freely,' said Funk. 'I was also jammed in a specially constructed chair, in a cramped position. For half a day I was whipped around the head.'

Lieutenant Rod Wells, the 23-year-old Australian who had built the radio receiver, ended up disabled for life following one interrogation session. 'The interviewer produced a small piece of wood like a meat skewer,' recalled Wells, 'pushed that into my left ear, and tapped it in with a small hammer. I think I fainted some time after it went through the drum. I remember the last excruciating sort of pain, and I must have gone out for some time because I was revived with a bucket of water. Eventually it healed but of course I couldn't hear with it. I have never been able to hear since.'[14]

Captain Matthews and the others managed to find the strength to resist all Japanese efforts to make them cough up the names of the other people in their organisation. In the end, all the Japanese had by way of evidence was the 'crime' of possession of an illegal wireless set and some vague notion that these men had been plotting against the occupation forces and distributing news bulletins. Matthews 'steadfastly refused to make admissions under brutal torture, beatings and starvation to implicate or endanger the lives of his associates'[15] commented the Australian investigation into his fate. The *Kempeitai* arrested and tortured fifty-two civilians and twenty POWs, accounting for virtually Matthews's entire network and a good proportion of the local underground as well.

All those arrested ended up in Kuching where they were sent for trial. Lieutenant Gordon Weynton was found guilty of 'spreading rumours' and sentenced to ten years imprisonment. Lieutenant Wells received twelve years hard labour, to be served in solitary confinement. Both officers were transported to Outram Road Jail in Singapore to serve out their sentences. This move undoubtedly saved them from the Sandakan Death Marches in 1945 and both men survived the war more or less in one piece. As for Lionel Matthews, his fate was sealed the moment he was captured. The court sentenced him to death by firing squad.

On 2 March 1944, alongside eight of the other ringleaders, Lionel Matthews faced his execution with great courage. 'He left Australia nearly 16 stone and he was only 6 stone at the end'[16] said his son David of the father he never knew. Captain Matthews declined a blindfold and looked his Japanese executioners square in the face at the moment of his death. He was posthumously awarded the George Cross for his courage and resourcefulness in captivity, the highest award available to Commonwealth citizens for valour that was not performed in battle.

For those men remaining in the Sandakan camps, almost every one of them would perish before the Japanese surrender. Small wonder that Sandakan stands today as a monument to Japanese barbarism, and Captain Lionel Matthews a monument to hope where no hope was supposed to exist.

Chapter 5

Ten Escape from Tojo

We were to see and experience a daily pattern of existence and treatment which will remain with us as nightmares and revolting memories for the rest of our lives.

Commander Melvin McCoy, USN

Lieutenant General Masaharu Homma's 14th Army began landing on Batan Island on the northern coast of Luzon, Philippines, on 8 December 1941, the same day that Japanese forces attacked Malaya and Hong Kong. Two days later more Japanese came ashore at Camiguin Island and at Vigan, Aparri and Gonzaga in northern Luzon, followed by another landing at Legazpi in southern Luzon on the 12th. On 19 December the island of Mindanao was attacked, and the US Asiatic Fleet withdrew after Japanese air attacks had devastated its important naval facilities at Cavite. With the US Pacific Fleet devastated at Pearl Harbor, the prospects for a successful American defence of the Philippines were not good.

General Homma's main assault began on 22 December when over 43,000 Japanese troops, well supported by artillery and armour, came ashore at Luzon's Lingayen Gulf. Approximately 120,000 Japanese faced a joint American-Filipino army of 150,000 troops, but the Filipinos, who made up the majority of General Douglas MacArthur's manpower, were badly trained, ill equipped and largely inexperienced. They were facing battle-hardened Japanese soldiers fresh from their campaigns in China who enjoyed complete air superiority and vital armoured support. Many of MacArthur's units were still mounted on horses. The American deputy commander, Lieutenant General Jonathan Wainwright, was unable to prevent the Japanese from landing, and forces under Major General George Parker that were supposed to block the road to the capital Manila were scattered by the strong enemy assault. The Japanese began to drive towards Manila virtually unopposed as thousands of refugees took to the roads and Japanese aircraft bombed and strafed both military and civilian targets mercilessly.

Japanese forces approached Manila at the end of December and MacArthur ordered the city garrison to evacuate. Most of MacArthur's forces surrendered or were overrun and captured as the Japanese drove away from the beaches towards the Filipino capital. The US Philippine Division covered the withdrawal of all remaining units into the Bataan Peninsula beside Manila Bay. On Boxing Day, MacArthur activated a prewar plan to defend only Bataan and Corregidor Island in the Bay, a plan that smacked of desperation. It looked as though the mighty United States was going to lose the Philippines entirely, something that had seemed impossible only two months before.

Throughout January 1942 the Japanese launched limited assaults into the Bataan perimeter, which was held by a mixture of Filipino and American forces. MacArthur's army was trapped and it was slowly ground down in combat. Supplies began to run short because the US Navy was unable to help the trapped army, and Japanese air superiority ruled out any attempt to evacuate the army from the Bataan Peninsula in a Far Eastern Dunkirk. President Franklin D. Roosevelt eventually ordered General MacArthur to leave. The order was against MacArthur's wishes, but General Wainwright assumed command on 12 March knowing full well that he would eventually become a POW. Roosevelt wanted to save MacArthur and his staff because he saw him leading the American fight back across the Pacific – allowing him to molder away in some Japanese POW camp was not the best use for MacArthur's talents.

Beginning on 28 March 1942, General Homma launched a series of strong attacks against the Allied line at Bataan, and despite fierce and dogged resistance, the Japanese managed to break through on 3 April, with many of Wainwright's units being overrun and scattered. American and Filipino troops were generally in a bad way, as the Bataan siege had taken its toll on their health. Apart from numerous combat casualties, most of Wainwright's troops were starving as supplies ran out, and sick with a plethora of untreated tropical diseases. Most were in a pitiful state compared with the British and Commonwealth troops taken at Singapore. This led to a major humanitarian disaster once they were in Japanese hands.

Wainwright's last stand occurred on the bastion of Corregidor Island in Manila Bay. In the years before the war the Army Corps of Engineers had excavated an extensive tunnel system beneath the island and into this labyrinthine world poured the retreating American and Filipino forces from the mainland. The island was a US Army Coast Artillery Post, and the anti-aircraft regiments stationed up above shot down dozens of Japanese aircraft during the siege. Many individuals augmented the American and Filipino Scouts garrison and units that had managed to get out of Bataan before the surrender and crossed the two miles of water to the island safely. Eventually, the Americans assembled approximately 11,000 troops with which to defend Corregidor. The Japanese began immediate preparations for an amphibious invasion of the island once they had pounded it into submission with bombers.

Meanwhile, in early April 1942, thousands of troops were being forced onto the infamous Bataan Death March after the exhausted, starving and demoralised defenders of the Bataan Peninsula had surrendered. 'We were to see Americans so crazed by thirst that they were forced to drink from muddy and polluted carabao wallows, although separated from the clean water of a running stream only by the menace of Japanese bayonets,' wrote a group of American officers who survived and eventually escaped from Japanese custody. Like spectators in hell, senior American officers were powerless to prevent endless Japanese atrocities from being committed against their men. 'We were to see unconscious Americans, exhausted on the march, tossed into shallow graves and buried while still alive,'[1] they wrote in 1944.

The Japanese forced the American and Filipino soldiers to march seventy-five miles in extreme heat from the Bataan perimeter to San Fernando, Pampanga. All of the men had been on short rations before surrender, and a high percentage were sick or wounded. Any man who fell out of the nine-day march was shot or bayoneted by the Japanese guards. Some were dragged from the column and beaten or tortured to death for the guards' amusement. For the first five days the Japanese distributed no food to the prisoners, and neither did they allow the men access to clean water. Instead, the prisoners were forced to drink from the muddy and diseased carabao wallows and ditches. Most then contracted severe dysentery as a result. 'My friend Sergeant Jones had a severe case of dysentery caused by drinking the muddy carabao wallow water,' recalled Staff Sergeant Samuel Moody. 'When he fell to the rear due to his condition he was beaten and struck with a bayonet. Later he died from his wounds.'[2]

On the sixth day of the march a Japanese military interpreter announced that the Japanese would feed the men if they would hand over all watches, rings and other remaining valuables. There were few valuables left as each man had been expertly 'frisked' by thieving Japanese soldiers when they were initially taken prisoner on Bataan. However, the Japanese issued each man with one teacup full of rice that evening. On the ninth day of the march the men received the welcome news that they would be taken to their prison camp, Camp O'Donnell, by train. The route that they had come was strewn with the bullet-riddled and bayoneted corpses of at least 8,000 American and Filipino soldiers. Over one hundred prisoners had been murdered on each mile of the Bataan Death March. More men died of suffocation on the train journey to O'Donnell as the Japanese packed the prisoners into the carriages so tightly than many could not breathe.

Some people were able to emulate General MacArthur and get away before the Japanese took Corregidor. In March 1942 the US Navy managed to get a few submarines through to the north side of Corregidor Island. They brought with them orders for General Wainwright, mail for the troops and more weapons. They left with an assortment of important passengers and cargo that included Filipino President Manuel Quezon along with hundreds of top government officials. Accompanying the civilians were several top American officers. Gold and silver bullion was also evacuated, along with stacks of important records. No place was found for eighty US Army nurses, who continued to work in the hospital beneath Malinta Hill and faced an uncertain fate in Japanese hands after the surrender.

The Japanese slowly and methodically wore down Corregidor's defences, eventually silencing all of the coast defence guns that prevented Japanese ships and landing craft from approaching the island. On the night of 5–6 May 1942, two Japanese infantry battalions stormed ashore on the northeast of the island in a surprise amphibious assault and quickly overwhelmed ferocious American resistance to establish a beachhead. General Homma rapidly expanded his beachhead by landing more troops, along with light tanks and artillery. The defenders were then slowly pushed back towards the island's highest point, the honeycombed Malinta Hill.

On 6 May General Wainwright asked General Homma for terms. Two days later Wainwright formally surrendered all of his remaining forces in the Philippines to the Japanese. The American defence had lasted six months longer than General Arthur Percival's muddled efforts to defend Malaya and Singapore.

When Corregidor Island fell to the Japanese another 9–10,000 American and Filipino personnel were taken prisoner. Among this group was Lieutenant Commander Melvin McCoy, US Navy, who along with many of his fellow Corregidor survivors was later sent to the notorious Cabanatuan POW camps, where the Japanese continued to torture, starve and murder the prisoners with impunity. McCoy and a small group of fellow American officers and men decided to escape at the first possible opportunity.

Cabanatuan POW camp was located seventy-five miles north of Manila. Surrounded by agricultural land, the camp was set out as a long rectangle measuring 500 by 700 yards, bounded on one of the shorter sides by a road to nearby Cabanatuan City and on the other three by scruffy, unkempt fields.

The first group of prisoners to arrive was those who had been taken prisoner after the fall of Corregidor in May 1942. On 27 May, after three weeks of brutal imprisonment in temporary facilities, the Japanese decided to transport them to Cabanatuan. 'It was their custom when American prisoners were to be moved, the

Japanese waited until the heat had reached its peak before loading some fifteen hundred of us into iron boxcars,' recalled Major Stephen Mellnik of the US Coast Artillery. 'There were a hundred men to each car, with no room to sit or lie down. The cars were tightly closed so that there was no ventilation. With the sun beating down on the metal roof, the inside of the car was like an oven, with no water or sanitary facilities available.'[3]

The final part of the journey to Cabanatuan was made on foot. 'When the sun had reached its zenith, we began our march of twelve miles to our prison camp,' wrote Mellnik. 'Not one of us was fit for marching. For five months we had been under siege on Corregidor, under constant strain. During more than three weeks of captivity the Japanese had not provided us with a single decent meal. Many of us were ill.'[4] Both on this march, and during the more infamous and bloody Bataan Death March, American prisoners noted the concern and many kindnesses of the local Filipinos, who often risked the wrath of the Japanese guards to try and offer some assistance. 'As we passed small Philippine barrios, or villages, on the march, the inhabitants seemed anxious to help us,' recounted Mellnik. 'Small children darted to our side and gave us balls of boiled rice. Those that were caught by the guards, however, were cuffed unmercifully.'[5] The Japanese brutally executed many Filipino civilians who tried to help the prisoners. 'A young woman, about twenty ... was caught hiding in the grass. The officer in command of the Japanese patrol which discovered her tore off all her clothes while two soldiers held her ... the officer with his sabre cut off her breasts and cut open her womb. Soldiers held her while the officer did this. At first the girl screamed but finally lay silent and still ...'[6]

The weary survivors dragged themselves into the camp on 29 May, many among them having perished beside the dusty road. Incredibly, and even though the prisoners were exhausted and in very low spirits, some among them were already contemplating escape. It was obvious to everyone that as long as one remained in Japanese captivity, the chances of surviving the war were slim indeed. Better to escape early whilst mind, body and spirit were still relatively intact than months down the line when starvation, illness and brutality would have taken their toll.

To a trio of US Navy men among the Corregidor prisoners, the time to escape was before the Japanese had become properly organised. 'The next morning [30 May 1942] the camp was electrified by a report which quickly swept through our ranks,' recalled Mellnik. 'During the night three young Naval Reserve ensigns had simply walked off into the darkness of the jungle and had successfully escaped. We were to hear more from these men later; and the Japanese lost no time in discovering which of the three prisoners were missing.'[7]

Judging by the attitude of local Filipinos towards the American POWs during the forced marches, it was obvious that the loyalties of most Filipinos were with the Americans. There would soon exist friendly local resistance groups who would endeavour to help escaped POWs make it to their own lines. Small numbers of US troops had also remained free and were acting as stay-behind parties as well, in a similar way to SOE in and around Hong Kong. Escape in the Philippines offered probably the best chance of survival compared with any other location in Occupied Asia except China.

The Japanese moved swiftly to prevent any further escape attempts. 'Barbed wire was hastily thrown about the camp, and sentry towers were built at short intervals,' wrote Major Mellnick. 'Then the grim Japs went through the camp and formed us off into groups of ten. If any one member of any group escaped, we were told, the other nine would be shot. These squads quickly became known among ourselves as "shooting squads", and each prisoner counted himself a member of his own "shooting squad".'[8] The prison stockade was split crosswise into three sections (groups), each about 230 yards wide. McCoy and Mellnik were housed inside group 1, the section nearest to the dusty road. Each group contained barracks for around 2,000 US prisoners, mostly officers and a few enlisted men. The majority of the enlisted prisoners were held at the separate Cabanatuan Camp No. 2 that was located six miles into the nearby jungle.

The arrival of the survivors of the Bataan Death March was an indescribable shock to the prisoners already at Cabanatuan. 'We had barely settled into the prison at Cabanatuan when, on June 2nd, the first detachments of prisoners from Bataan began to arrive at our camp,' said Mellnick. 'We were appalled at their condition, and even more appalled when we learned what had happened to them on what they all called "the death march from Bataan".' Instead of marching to Cabanatuan, the Bataan survivors arrived in trucks 'for the simple reason that only a very few among them were physically able to stand up and walk a hundred yards.'[9]

Mellnik was appalled when he discovered in the first truck a young enlisted man who had once served as his orderly. 'He staggered to my side and, holding himself up by feebly grasping at my shoulders, he sobbed out, "Sir, is it different here – will they treat us like humans?" I tried to comfort the boy by telling him that everything would be all right, and he staggered away, still sobbing,' wrote Mellnik. 'The Bataan prisoners who were joining us now, and who had been prisoners a month longer than we had, were the most woe-begone objects I have ever seen,' noted a furious Mellnik. 'They were wild-eyed, gaunt, their clothes in tatters. Many had no equipment of any kind, and some clutched at rusty tin cans which they used as mess kits. These men had their own doctors with them – the medical detachments from Bataan – but the doctors had no medicines, and they were as sick as the men.'[10] What was starkly clear was that it would not be too long before all of the POWs at Cabanatuan were reduced to the same sick and enfeebled condition by Japanese neglect. Escape appeared the only solution.

Mellnik had arrived at Cabanatuan well before McCoy. 'Mellnik had been at Cabanatuan about five weeks when I learned that I also was to be transferred there,' recalled McCoy. 'After being captured on Corregidor, I had spent my first few days at Pasay, where the Japs had turned an elementary school into a prison for the senior Army and Navy staff officers. When these officers were removed from Pasay – presumably to be taken to prisons in Japan or Formosa – I was transferred to Old Bilibid in Manila.' The new regime McCoy and the other officers experienced was an eye-opener, to say the least. 'At Old Bilibid I was assigned to such jobs as cleaning out Japanese latrines and sewage systems,' recalled a disgusted McCoy. 'On another occasion I took a detail of enlisted men, under heavy guard, to Rizal Stadium, where the Japs had concentrated mountains of captured American quartermaster supplies. Much of these supplies consisted of food, and the Japs told us as we loaded it on trucks that it was to be sent to the American prisoners of war. During my eleven months of captivity I was never to see any of this food. In fact, and except for boiled rice, I was never to see much food of any kind.'

McCoy arrived at Cabanatuan Camp on 7 July 1942. 'My first impression of Cabanatuan was one of utter desolation and hopelessness. As I was mustered into the camp I was first searched by Japanese guards. The only things of value they found on me were two small bottles containing quinine and sulfa drugs, which had been given me by a doctor friend at Old Bilibid,' wrote McCoy. 'The Japs confiscated this medicine.'[11]

On arrival at Cabanatuan McCoy fell into conversation with a Bataan survivor named Major Gunn. Gunn's response to most questions put forward by McCoy was 'you won't like it here'. Aside from the camp's obvious deficiencies in food, accommodation and medical supplies, Gunn warned McCoy about the Japanese guards. ' "You won't like it here," said Major Gunn. I followed his eyes. A platoon of Japanese troops and an officer were swinging down the road toward the camp, singing a marching song,' recalled McCoy. 'Rumour in the camp had it that this group had guerillas. We soon saw that the rumour was correct. The platoon marched in military order up to our stockade and halted on an order from the officer. Then they impaled a gory Filipino head on a tall fence post near our gate.' The message was clear, both to the POW population and to any potential escapees among it. 'This obviously was a subtle warning against any infraction of our prison rules. We were soon to learn that it was not an empty threat.'[12]

'At the north end of our rectangle was a moat which occasionally filled with water during heavy rains, and which we used for drainage for our latrines and urinals,' recalled McCoy. 'Nearly always in this section were to be found a number of prisoners dead or dying of dysentery and starvation, men who had made it this far and could go no further.' McCoy was able to record much of what he saw, and his words would eventually find their way to the Oval Office and the desk of President Roosevelt himself. 'We were to see Americans by the hundred suffering in various declining stages of scurvy, malaria, beri beri and other afflictions, because the Japanese would not give us our medications, which

85

they had confiscated; neither would the Japanese permit us to use the fruits and vegetables which grew in profusion around our prison stockade.' A deliberate lack of food caused terrible suffering among the POWs, as the Japanese intended. 'We were to see Americans slowly going blind from vitamin deficiency; and not one of us escaped without having suffered from one or more diseases and deficiencies which at one time were causing the deaths of more than 50 Americans each day.'[13]

Casual brutality became every American prisoner's daily companion, to add to the twin miseries of starvation and illness. 'We were to see American prisoners slapped and beaten without provocation as a commonplace occurrence, and most of us were the helpless personal recipients of such treatment,' wrote McCoy. 'We were to see Americans tied up and tortured in full view of our prison camp, beaten and battered until they were no longer recognizable as human beings, before they were finally removed for execution without trial.'

McCoy, Major Stephen Mellnik, and eight other men decided that they must escape from the Cabanatuan hellhole, or die trying. 'There was little choice for the ten of us who finally escaped from the Japanese,' wrote McCoy. 'We knew that if we were caught in the attempt we would be put to death in a manner not pleasant to think about – we had seen it happen to others of our American prisoners.'[14] But if they stayed, most, if not all of them, would probably have died from disease and starvation.

Meanwhile, following the first successful escape from Cabanatuan by the three naval ensigns on 30 May 1942 (mentioned above) other prisoners decided to attempt to get away. The second successful escapee was a Mexican soldier who was serving in the US Army. 'One enlisted man from the 200th Coast Artillery escaped from the hospital in late July or early August. This man, a Mexican, went to Cabanatuan and, passing as a Filipino, worked for the Japs,' recalled Mellnik. 'Our grapevine soon informed him that the other nine men of his squad had been marked for execution, so he voluntarily returned and gave himself up.' The Japanese made an example of this soldier as a warning to the others not to escape. 'This man was first beaten by the guards, then shackled loosely so he could walk. Then he was put on permanent latrine duty, and was always followed by a guard who held a rope which was tied around the prisoner. At night he was locked up,'[15] wrote Mellnik.

The Japanese, despite becoming increasingly paranoid about escape attempts, also made mistakes. 'There was another flurry in early August when the Japs reported that two prisoners had escaped from the hospital,' recorded Mellnik. 'The "shooting squads" of these men were immediately isolated for execution, and the execution date was set, when the bodies of the men who had supposedly escaped were fortunately discovered. One had fallen into a latrine, and the body of another was found behind a barracks. Both apparently had been delirious when they died.'[16] On another occasion five enlisted men were caught in the act of bartering food with two Filipinos through the camp's perimeter wire. The Japanese arrested all seven men. The Japanese were concerned lest the Filipinos had told the Americans anything about the progress of the war, and whether the Americans had been trying to foment anti-Japanese resistance among the locals. Events were to take a tragically violent turn. 'The five Americans and two Filipinos, as punishment, were tied up to stakes just out-side the camp and allowed no food or water for forty-eight hours,' wrote Mellnik. 'In tying one of the Americans, the Japanese guards had done a bungling job, and this man finally found that he could wriggle out of his bonds. The midday heat was almost unbearable. At about noon of the second day, this enlisted man apparently became crazed by the combination of heat, hunger and thirst.' Jerking himself free of his bonds, he ran to the stockade gate and let himself in. 'Once inside his own Barracks he got some water and then went to his own bunk and lay down.' Although this prisoner later ran back inside the prison stockade, the Japanese charged him with attempted escape. 'At about five o'clock that afternoon all of us were herded into our barracks under guard. The barracks were so flimsily constructed, however, that it was impossible to prevent the prisoners from seeing what went on outside,' recalled Mellnik. 'Those prisoners who were near enough thus could look through the chinks in their barracks as the Japanese lined up the five Americans and two Filipinos and executed them by rifle fire. There was no trial.'[17]

Incredibly, for the first three months of its existence Japanese non-commissioned officers commanded Cabanatuan Camp, showing just how unimportant and low status Allied POWs were to the Imperial Army. Eventually, the Japanese placed an officer in charge. To the further amazement of the prisoners they chose a Japanese bicycle shop owner from Manila named Mori who was given a temporary commission as a lieutenant colonel. 'Butter wouldn't melt in his mouth,' recalled one enlisted prisoner. 'He couldn't be nice enough to us guys in uniform.' A shipment of quinine was distributed and for a while it looked as though the high death rate from malaria would decrease. Perhaps Colonel Mori, a civilian in uniform, was a decent man. 'The death rate among the American prisoners dropped from 30 per day in July to 21 per day in August, principally due to the fact that many of the weaker ones had already died,' wrote Mellnik. 'September showed an all-time low of 14 per day, but this rose to 19 per day in October. By the middle of October the small supply of quinine had been used up, and deaths from malaria were on the increase.' The death rate remained appallingly high. 'At the time I left Cabanatuan in October 1942, being transferred to another camp, approximately 3,000 persons had died there,' wrote Mellnik. 'Twenty-two hundred had died earlier at Camp O'Donnell, not counting the unknown number killed by the Japanese or who died on the death march from Bataan. This makes a known total of more than 5,000 Americans dead by October, 1942.'[18] As well as the American deaths, 27,000 Filipino troops had perished in captivity since the Bataan Death March in April 1942. One National Guard regiment that had begun the war with 1,000 men had lost 25 killed and 75 missing in action before the 6 May surrender. But a further 453 of the men died in Japanese captivity.

The Japanese eventually recaptured the three naval ensigns who had boldly walked out of Cabanatuan Camp on the first night of their imprisonment. They were sent back to Cabanatuan and paraded before the rest of the prisoners. The Japanese forced them to relate their stories as a lesson for the assembled POWs. The ensigns had spent three months hiding in the jungle. Food had been plentiful and they stated that they could have remained there indefinitely. However, they were determined to escape from the Philippines, and this is where they had come unstuck. 'They made their way to the more thickly populated coast of the island of Luzon. The Japanese were in force on the coast, and the penalty for a Filipino harboring an American was death,' said Mellnik. 'In fact, even a suspicion was enough to cause a Filipino to be executed. The three ensigns decided that without help escape would be hopeless, so they voluntarily turned themselves in.'[19]

Stephen Mellnik witnessed the arrival of the naval officers in camp. 'That evening after our meal, and while it was still dark, these three young officers were required to mount a platform in the center of the camp and read prepared statements about the hardships they had undergone while they were away from the camp. They told of weeks without food, of jungle water infested with bugs and poisonous insects, of venomous snakes and ferocious wild beasts.' Mellnik and the other POWs knew that these statements were blatantly untrue. 'Actually, none of the Americans in the camp was fooled,' he wrote. 'The ensigns had been beaten up when they first gave themselves up, but beyond their bruises they looked better than any prisoner in the camp. They were occasionally cuffed around by the guards after their return, but theirs was the mildest punishment given out by the Japs during all my months in prison.'[20] Like the Black Death, Japanese military 'justice' occasionally spared those who under most circumstances should have expected terminal treatment.

A very different fate awaited another trio of officers who escaped from Cabanatuan in September 1942, a fate that clearly demonstrated the schizophrenic nature of the Japanese military mind. Two US Army lieutenant colonels and a naval lieutenant made an attempt on a very dark night by crawling along a ditch and then through the perimeter wire. Each man was armed with a homemade club. They had almost reached their objective when their progress was accidentally halted; 'an army enlisted man, said to have been a former Notre Dame football star, stumbled into the three men in the dark,' recalled McCoy. 'Whatever his reasons, one of the lieutenant colonels sprang from the ditch and laid about the enlisted man with his club. Other Americans ran out of their barracks to stop this fray, with the result that it became general and quite noisy.' Once the fighting stopped, the first lieutenant colonel loudly proclaimed that there had been a deliberate attempt inside the camp to prevent his escape. 'The enlisted man denied this, and since he was not a member of the officer's "shooting squad", and so would not have suffered from the escape, he presumably was sincere in his denial,' wrote McCoy.

The word 'escape' was used so many times that the Japanese eventually got to hear about the most recent attempt. The three American officers were taken out of the camp, and after some questioning by the Japanese, their punishment was decided upon. 'The Japanese first beat the three Americans about the feet and calves until they were no longer able to stand,' said McCoy. 'Then they kicked the men and jumped on them with all their weight. After an extended example of this treatment, the Japanese waited until morning and then stripped the Americans of all their clothing except their shorts. The three men were then marched out into the Cabanatuan road to a point which was in full view of the camp,' recalled a horrified McCoy. 'Their hands were tied behind them, and they were pulled up by ropes from an overhead purchase so that they had to remain standing, but bent forward to ease the pressure on their arms.' The Japanese thus tortured the three American officers for a further two days. 'Many of the prisoners went into their barracks so they would not be able to see what went on,' said McCoy. 'The Japanese guards were ready with their sub-machine guns in case of any trouble. The Japanese periodically beat the men with a heavy board. Any Filipino unlucky enough to pass along the road was forced to strike the men in the face with this club. If the Japanese did not think the Filipinos put enough force into their blows, the Filipinos themselves were beaten.'

Incredibly, the three American officers somehow clung on to life under this appalling abuse. 'They were battered beyond recognition, with the ear of one prisoner hanging down to his shoulder,' wrote McCoy. 'I think we all prayed for the men during this ordeal. I know I did. And I am sure all of us said a prayer of relief when the Japanese finally cut the men down and took them away for execution. Two of the men were shot. The third was beheaded. There had at no time been a semblance of a trial.'

At the end of September 1942 the Japanese announced that they were transferring two large groups of prisoners away from

Cabanatuan. A first party, numbering 400 technicians, was selected from among the prisoners and shipped out to Japan, and thence on to Manchuria where the men were employed as labourers down local salt mines. A second party numbering 1,000 men, including McCoy and Mellnik, was sent south to the Philippine island of Mindanao. 'At the time of the transfer of prisoners from Cabanatuan none of us had as yet formed any clear plan of escape, although it was always in our minds,' wrote McCoy. 'There were less than 200 Navy and Marine Corps personnel in the camp, as against some 8,000 Army, so a portion of our number was allowed to volunteer to go to the new camp. I was one of the volunteers.' McCoy thought that he was lucky to have been selected. 'I was convinced that staying at Cabanatuan meant eventual death; although I was one of the healthiest specimens in the camp, in five months I had already lost eighteen pounds,' he wrote. 'Therefore I was doubly glad I had volunteered when, in some inexplicable manner, word got around that we were to be sent to a prison colony on Mindanao, the furthest southward of the Philippine Islands, and about 600 statute miles on a direct line from Cabanatuan.'

On 26 October 1942 the 1,000-man party went to Manila and boarded a 7,000-ton former British freighter for the eleven-day voyage to Mindanao. 'We were loaded into two holds of the ship, but since there was not room for all hands, a number of us were placed on the unprotected deck,' recalled McCoy. 'I was one of the lucky ones topside, while Mellnik was in the almost unbearably crowded confines of a cargo hold.' Captain William Dyess recalled: 'I think it must have been the filthiest vessel ever to put to sea ... The hold in which we were to sleep smelled almost as bad as the hospitals at O'Donnell and Cabanatuan prison camps.'[21] At noon each day the Japanese distributed decent quality boiled rice, this time enlivened with a little dried fish. And at dinner the prisoners received a morsel of tinned corned beef that the Japanese had captured from the Cavite Navy Yard. 'Except for a few with money, none of us had tasted meat in months, or little else that was substantial,' wrote McCoy. 'I can remember how those of us on deck turned this tit-bit over in our mouths and luxuriated in the taste.'

The rusting freighter finally tied up at a lumber pier near Davao City on the morning of 8 November. Once unloaded, the Japanese forced the American POWs to march seventeen miles through the hottest time of the day to Davao Penal Colony. This former Philippine prison had been emptied of most of its civilian inmates by the Japanese, with the exception of 150 convicts who were kept on to help run the prison farm. 'As we marched into the prison colony we were lined up for review by Major Maida, the Japanese prison commander,' wrote Mellnik. 'We could see that he was furious. Major Maida pointed at the great number in our ranks who were so ill they could barely stand. He stormed about, declaring that he had asked for prisoners capable of doing hard labour. Instead, he shouted, he had been sent a batch of walking corpses.' Lieutenant Colonel Mori, the commandant of Cabanatuan Camp, had clearly got rid of those prisoners who were most likely to die in his camp by shipping them off to Davao.

Major Maida stood before the American prisoners and outlined in a loud voice their new duties. The work 'included planting and harvesting rice; the planting and harvesting of corn, camotes and mongo beans; logging; the building of field fortifications, barbed wire entanglements and parapets for riflemen; plowing, and the miscellaneous slavey work of keeping up the Japanese camp area, such as the latrine detail,' recalled Mellnik. Maida also added ominously: 'You have been used to a soft easy life since your capture. All that will be different here. Now you will learn about hard labour. Every prisoner will continue to work until he is actually hospitalised. Punishment for malingering will be severe.'

The Japanese brought in more American prisoners from other camps to bring the total up to 2,000. True to Maida's words, within five months 900 of these Americans were hospitalised because of overwork, disease and starvation.

The prisoners' primary nemesis at Davao was not Major Maida however, but his second-in-command, Lieutenant Hosume. The prisoners grew to fear and loathe this sadistic officer, nicknaming him 'The Crown Prince of Swat'. 'According to the Filipino convicts at the prison, Hosume had distinguished himself in a couple of actions by doing his fighting at the rear,' wrote Mellnik. 'As a punishment, he was assigned to the prison detail at Davao, and he seemed bent on proving his bravery by smacking around every American prisoner in reach.'

The Filipino convicts were kept on at Davao by the Japanese so that they could gain remission for their capital crimes by teaching the POWs how to be hard workers. As remission was an empty promise the convicts instead became fast friends with the Americans and taught them how to appear to do a lot while actually doing very little. The convicts were also not averse to settling scores with particular Japanese guards, something no POW would have even contemplated. Fighter pilot Dyess was on a work detail one day with a Filipino convicted murderer. Their guard had had this Filipino tied and flogged a few weeks previously for selling leaf tobacco to American prisoners. The guard called a rest period, took off his boots and settled down underneath the shade of a tree. 'With a spring so swift it made him look like a little brown blur, the Filipino seized an ax and buried it in the Jap's neck, almost decapitating him,' recalled Dyess. 'Then he snatched a bolo knife and executed some intricate and pretty shocking carving on the remains.'[22] Pulling on the dead Japanese guard's boots, the Filipino snatched up his rifle and without looking back ran off into the jungle. Dyess and the other POWs were not harmed when the Japanese discovered what had happened, apparently treating the murder as a purely Filipino-Japanese quarrel.

Although conditions at Davao were slightly better than those encountered at Cabanatuan, several of the prisoners were determined to escape at the first opportunity. 'Almost since the day of arrival at Mindanao there had been lurking in my mind the thought of escape, the hope that some avenue would open itself, that some opportunity would be provided,' wrote McCoy. 'Nothing concrete came of these gropings all through November and December. There were the usual six days of work each week, with Sunday quite often thrown in as a work day when Lieutenant Hosume caught us stealing food.' Then, in early January 1943, McCoy was assigned as officer-in-charge of a detail to work at the prison's coffee plantation. The detail consisted of thirty-five officers all over the age of forty who were mostly lieutenant colonels. 'These older men had been assigned to this detail as a result of considerable undercover maneuvering on the part of the American officials of the prison, in order that they might have a better chance of stealing food enough to keep them alive,' wrote McCoy. Mellnik was also assigned to this detail, making himself and McCoy the youngest men assigned. They immediately began planning an escape.

'At Mellnik's suggestion we wangled two sergeants to assist with the mid-day cooking for our work party – Sergeants Paul Marshall and R.B. Spielman,' recalled McCoy. 'Marshall and Spielman were taken in on the escape plan, and at once proved both eager and helpful. Our hope was to make a break out of the prison farm, elude our guards, reach the coast, and set out in a stolen sailboat.' Both McCoy and Mellnik were aware that their chances were slim. 'We were not too enthusiastic about our chances for a successful escape. On the other hand, neither were we too enthusiastic about our chances for staying alive if we remained in the hands of the Japs.'

The escape plan was interrupted in January 1943 by the sudden and dramatic distribution of Red Cross parcels by the Japanese, a virtually unheard of luxury. 'The news was true,' recalled McCoy, who had first heard a rumour from a navy storeman he had served with. 'There were, indeed, Red Cross boxes, and two for each prisoner. More than that, they meant to each of us – home. As each prisoner ripped open a box, I suspect that there were many besides myself who worked with a catch in the throat.' These cardboard boxes filled with precious and scarce commodities appeared heaven-sent to the desperate American prisoners. 'First of all, there was coffee – a concentrate which tasted better than any steaming cup I had ever drunk to cheer an icy night on the bridge of a ship at sea,' wrote McCoy. 'It was the first I had tasted since a smuggled sip in Old Bilibid Prison, back in Manila. There were chocolate bars, there was cheese, there were tinned meats and sardines, there were cigarettes, and there was a portion each of tea, cocoa, salt, pepper and sugar. Best of all, there were sulfa drugs and precious quinine!' McCoy was overjoyed, as were all of the prisoners. 'Our Christmas had been delayed, but it was one of the most enjoyable many of us will ever remember.' The Japanese also issued fifteen cans of corned beef or meat-and-vegetable stew to each prisoner, distributed at a rate of two cans a week.

By March 1943 the Red Cross food had been exhausted, and the men were thrown back onto a poor prison camp diet of watery rice and weeds. However, McCoy and Mellnik's escape plans were well advanced. '"How far is it to Australia from here, Commander?" Sergeant Marshall asked me one day, while we were out on the coffee detail,' recalled McCoy.

'"About sixteen hundred miles to one of the nearest points," I answered. "Melville, for instance."

'"And you mean, if we can find a sailboat, you can take us there?"

'"Within ten or fifteen miles of any place on the map. Provided, of course, that we can rig up some half-way decent navigating equipment." And provided, of course, that we had a lot of luck with the weather, and the Japs didn't stop us. But I kept these thoughts to myself.'

'McCoy, as senior officer, was to lead our escape group, and was to do the navigating once we were able to steal a boat,' recalled Mellnik. 'When, and if, we reached the coast and could steal a boat. Meanwhile, I was doing much of the planning, and was responsible for executing most of the preparatory detail.'

To give themselves the best chance of making a successful escape, the Americans realised that they needed to improve their health. Months of starvation in Japanese hands had left them unfit and vulnerable to illness. Spielman proved to be a 'food thief deluxe' and the group targeted the Japanese chicken farm that contained upwards of 3,000 fowl. 'We made it a point of honour never to take less than two on a single raid, and including as many eggs as could be safely carried,' said Mellnik. 'By an elaborate system of watchers, McCoy and Spielman and I relieved the Japs of a total of 133 of their plumpest fowls over a period of three months.' But the Japanese were not unaware of how inviting a target their chickens were proving. After Spielman and his fellow escapers had stolen seventy-five chickens, the Japanese began to take notice. Each subsequent theft required more guile and ingenuity. If any of the Americans were caught chicken rustling they faced dire punishments that ranged from a severe flogging to a possible death sentence. 'Some of these chickens we ate at the noon meal we cooked for ourselves while working in the coffee plantation, dividing them with the older officers in our work party,' said Mellnik. 'Others we traded for quinine, sulfa drugs and any other article which we considered might be useful on our trip through the jungle and onward to Australia.'

In early March 1943 Captain Austin 'Shifty' Shofner of the US Marine Corps approached McCoy with an idea. Shofner told McCoy that he and five other army and Marine Corps officers were planning their own escape, but they had decided to ask McCoy to take charge. McCoy agreed with the idea of merging the two groups into one large group of escapers that, in addition to Shofner, would include three US Army Air Corps fighter pilots: Captain Dyess, Second Lieutenant L.A. Boelens, and Second Lieutenant Samuel Grashio. The remaining two officers were Marine First Lieutenants Jack Hawkins and Michael Dobervich, 'both fearless, resourceful, dependable, and in fair physical condition,'[23] recalled Dyess. 'Our two groups now merged, and we added to our party two Filipino convicts who were serving time for murder, Beningno de la Cruz and Victorio Jumprung,' said McCoy. Sam Grashio 'had given up his job in the kitchen because he hated the Japs so much he could no longer trust himself in a spot where butcher knives were at hand,'[24] wrote Dyess.

At the new group's first meeting McCoy announced that he would need a sextant for navigation. 'Lieutenant Boelens said that he could make a sextant in the prison workshop. He not only kept his promise – he did a bang-up good job into the bargain,' wrote McCoy. 'In the same manner, Mellnik was able to lay his hands on a book on astronomy, and I was able to obtain the necessary data on the principal stars, and also the equation of time. We were also able to obtain the proper altitude corrections; and since I could compute the correct ascension and declination of the sun, I felt prepared to navigate within reasonable limits,' wrote McCoy. McCoy had a pocket watch which had a fairly constant rate 'and whose error I determined by comparing the watch with the time of apparent local noon. (I found, when finally I was able to get a time tick by radio, that I was only fifteen seconds off.)' Bolo knives were shortened into daggers, with some unaltered to use against jungle foliage, non-perishable food supplies traded for stolen chickens and a watch and compass stolen from the Japanese. With these instruments and their improved supply of food and medicines, the group was soon ready to depart. The escapers had not told anyone else about their plan, which was a wise precaution for there were always stool pigeons in any POW camp who were prepared to sell out their comrades in return for more food or cigarettes.

McCoy selected as the day for the escape Sunday 28 March 1943. This was because it was a day of rest and the Japanese would not discover that the men were missing for eight hours, giving the group a valuable head start. Conditions at the camp were deteriorating rapidly, spurring the escapers into action.

On 14 March the escapees carried out a dry run of the plan without equipment. They discovered that none of the guards in the watchtowers and observation posts could see them. On 26 March they started sneaking their escape equipment out of the camp and caching it in the nearby jungle. The Japanese were afraid of the Philippine jungle, which was crawling with heavily armed and aggressive guerrillas, and only entered fully armed and in force. 'The reason for this is the fact that very little is contributed to the New Order in East Asia by a Japanese with his head cut off,' wrote Mellnik.

On the following day the group continued sneaking out more equipment, but their route took them past the guardhouse. This was the one weakness in their plan. 'Captain Dyess remembered that the sentries at this guardhouse were very partial to the fruit which was gathered for use by the Japanese, and which usually was brought by this spot,' recalled McCoy. 'On the day before we planned to escape, we placed our equipment in the bottom of a bull cart driven by Dyess and Mellnik. The equipment was then hidden by covering it with a load of small logs. On the back of the cart was placed a burlap bag of star apples, such as was often delivered in this manner to the Japanese quartermaster.' When the cart came to a halt before the sentry, he 'took his usual rake-off of the star apples and waved the cart on. The equipment was safely hidden in the jungle.'

The worst moment came at another gate when a sentry stopped the cart again.

The group had unfortunately overlooked one other wildcard in the plan, the feared Lieutenant Hosume. Each morning the prisoners on work details received their lunch ration of rice to take with them. At noon on 27 March Hosume made an inspection to see if any of the prisoners was in possession of forbidden food, such as fruit and vegetables. Captain Shofner had the escape

97

group's entire supply of the anti-malarial drug quinine inside his lunch bag. 'Hosume opened the bag and looked in. The quinine was in plain view,' recalled Mellnik. 'Captain Shofner said later that he established a new world's record for holding the breath. Fortunately for us all, the Crown Prince of Swat had a one-track mind: he was looking for forbidden food and he saw none in the bag. After slapping around the men in Shofner's party, he continued on his honorable and exalted way.'

But Hosume wasn't quite done with them yet. Although the escapers had managed to move all of their equipment into the jungle without being caught, and they still planned to escape that Sunday, Lieutenant Hosume intervened in their escape plan. 'That night we received very disturbing news. Lieutenant Hosume had found forbidden food in possession of one of the work parties,' wrote Mellnik. 'As a general punishment, all hands were ordered to work in the rice fields the following day – the Sunday on which we were to have made our escape. Our equipment was hidden in the edge of the jungle, where it might be discovered at any moment by the Japanese, and thus give us away.' McCoy had no choice but to postpone their escape until the following Sunday, an agonising decision but a sensible one under the circumstances.

For seven days the eight military prisoners lived in a state of perpetual tension. Every time a Japanese guard approached one of them, they feared that their escape equipment had been discovered in the nearby jungle. 'As each day passed without discovery, each of us sent up a prayer of thanks. And each of us prayed that, on the coming Sunday, we would not be punished by an order to work. Our luck held,' wrote McCoy.

McCoy had set the new day of the escape for Sunday 4 April. But on the Thursday before the POWs noticed that the guards had suddenly become agitated and watchful. McCoy detailed Marshall to scout around and find out what was going on. Marshall soon returned with a warning. ' "We've got to watch our step," he said. "There was some trouble today. The Japs may be onto something," ' recalled McCoy.

' "What happened?"

' "Jap sentry shot down a hospital orderly. Said he was trying to escape."

' "Was he trying to escape?"

98

' "No, sir. We can't figure it out, unless maybe the damn Jap just had trigger itch." '

The hospital orderly, an enlisted man named McFee, had been digging camotes to supplement the hospital patients' meagre diet just outside the hospital stockade and almost directly beneath a Japanese guard tower. As it was an extremely hot day McFee called to a comrade inside the stockade to toss him over a canteen of water, which his comrade did. 'McFee was about to drink from the canteen when the Jap guard in the sentry tower suddenly yelled at him,' wrote Mellnik. 'Wondering at the commotion, and not understanding the words being shouted at him, McFee tilted the canteen and spilled some of the liquid to show the Japanese that it was nothing more than water. That was McFee's mistake, although we were never able to find out just why.' The Japanese guard shouted at McFee again, shouldered his rifle, took aim at the hapless American and fired.

'The bullet entered at the junction of the neck and shoulder and came out through the hip,' wrote Mellnik. 'McFee yelled out, as he staggered, "My God – don't shoot me again." The sentry poured two more bullets into McFee's body, and then fired the remaining shots in his clip at McFee's buddy inside the hospital compound, and who by this time was running for dear life for the safety of the barracks. This second man was not hit.'

The next day the Japanese camp commandant informed the senior American officers that McFee had been 'shot while trying to escape'. Then the matter was closed.

For Lieutenant Commander McCoy, the Friday and Saturday that followed McFee's shooting were among the longest days of his life. 'On Sunday morning I got up early and began to hide my home-made charts, extra clothing, medicines, etc., underneath my usual garments,' he recalled. 'Very carefully, I placed in an inner pocket three fragile pina cloth handkerchiefs which I had found in a tunnel on Corregidor on the day of surrender, and which I devoutly hoped I would some day be able to present to my wife, Betty Anne, and my two little daughters, Anne and Jean.' Underneath his clothing he stuffed his mosquito netting that would prove to be vital equipment in the jungle.

Captain Shofner was in charge of a ploughing party that used Indian steers. He had permission to leave the prison regularly to change the animals' grazing location, and on that Sunday morning he took with him Jack Hawkins and Michael Dobervich, as well as army pilot Samuel Grashio. McCoy faced more difficulty in getting his party, consisting of Mellnik, Dyess, Boelens, Spielman and Marshall, clear of the main prison compound. 'The first test to face us was the main gate, leading from the prison confines into the prison farm,' recalled McCoy. 'This we somehow passed safely, despite the bulky appearance caused by the articles hidden underneath our clothing.'

Once McCoy's party was out of view of the main gate they ducked into a nearby coconut grove and began to crawl towards a place where they had hidden their escape equipment in the jungle. Unfortunately, the group would have to cross a prison road that was always patrolled by a Japanese sentry. 'When we reached this spot we formed into ranks and marched boldly into view,' wrote McCoy. 'As we passed the sentry I called for "eyes left", and as the others complied I gave a snappy salute. This we never did except with an occasional guard who was a little less severe than the others; in payment for his kindness we thus attempted to give him "face" with his superiors.' The Japanese sentry was so surprised that he returned the Americans' salute and actually smiled as they marched past. Soon McCoy and Shofner's parties had successfully rendezvoused in the jungle and retrieved their equipment. After sitting out in the damp conditions for a week the escapers discovered that most of it was now useless.

The group waited quietly in the jungle for their two Filipino guides, Benigno de la Cruz and Victorio Jumarung. Of the two guides, only 'Victor' Jumarung had been in the jungle before, but after an hour of trekking he admitted that he was lost. After a hurried conference McCoy decided to navigate by compass alone. However, 'Ben' de la Cruz and Victor were still vital to the escape plan once contact was made with local Filipinos.

The trekking was appallingly difficult through the rain-soaked jungle. 'The rain continued to come down,' recalled Dyess. 'The ooze was knee deep and the dim path often dipped through water-filled gullies. There were mosquitos in the millions.'[25] The escapers had to slash a path through the thick foliage with their bolo knives. This meant that any pursuing force of Japanese would find them quickly for the escapers had already cut a path for them and left a very obvious trail. They checked their compass course every four or five minutes. 'The jungle heat was oppressive, the noise broken only by our own careful progress, the squawk of startled birds, or the chatter of occasional beady-eyed and elusive monkeys,' recalled Mellnik. 'Soon we were in swamp, with water up to our knees and in sharp-edged coogan grass that grew over our heads. We had to hack our way every step.'[26] Dyess recalled the swamp: 'The heat was steamy and weakening.'[27]

That first night of freedom was spent camping in water that was ankle-deep. The escapees kept dry by cutting down tree branches to fashion crude structures over the water. 'When we turned in all of us were near the point of exhaustion, and all of us slept the sleep of the dead,' wrote Mellnik. 'As a result, none of us aroused when the water rose during the night, and we awoke to find ourselves half-floating in our beds.' McCoy was showing signs of illness. 'It was a considerable task for him to summon enough strength during the day to keep himself from falling out – he said that, if this happened, he would expect the rest of us to go on. Somehow, he managed to keep going,' wrote Mellnik. On the second night, about 8pm, the group heard small arms fire and an explosion about two miles away that came from the direction of the camp. 'And, the next morning, McCoy's indisposition had cleared away without leaving him in the throes of dysentery or malaria, as we had feared.'[28]

The going was brutal – in four days of hacking and stumbling through the dense jungle the group had only managed to stagger twelve miles. 'And we soon found obvious evidence that the Japs had been on the hunt for us – evidence in the shape of an empty ammunition clip, and the remains of food which the Jap search party had eaten,' wrote Mellnik. What Mellnik did not mention was that he was in considerable discomfort after having cut his hand on his bolo knife whilst hacking through the thick foliage. It was a wound that would plague him for forty days. 'Our shoes were falling apart,' recalled Dyess. 'Our legs and bodies had been slashed severely by the sword grass. Infections would start swiftly.'[29] Even though the escapers were suffering miserably in the jungle and swamp, their morale was actually quite high. 'We always were able to thank God we were anywhere except back among the Japs, subject to their barbaric cruelties, their policy of systematic starvation, and their creed of murder for captives,' wrote Dyess in 1944. 'Even when things were at their worst we could say to ourselves that we were damn well off.'[30] Such sentiments were shared by all of the men in this book who chose to risk their lives in escape rather than tolerate any more abuse at the hands of the Japanese.

A first, and potentially fatal, contact was made with the Filipino resistance movement. 'On a morning while we were still at breakfast, Captain Dyess was standing guard when he saw two armed Filipinos,' recalled Mellnik. 'The Filipinos saw Dyess at the same time, and one of them made motions as if he had attempted to fire. Dyess called to the Filipinos, but they quietly faded into the jungle.' This strange encounter was eventually explained after the group made proper contact with the guerrillas that night. 'When finally we made contact with these guerrillas, they admitted that two of them had been the ones seen in the jungle by Dyess,' wrote Mellnik. 'They thought he was a Jap, they said; one of them had taken careful aim on Dyess and had pulled the trigger. Dyess owed his life to a faulty cartridge or firing pin.'[31]

The guerrillas told McCoy and the others that the Japanese were in the jungle in force and actively hunting the American escapees. Just a few hours before, the small guerrilla group of sixteen Filipinos had ambushed a company of Japanese that was eighty strong in the jungle, shooting down ten before the guerrillas had melted into the undergrowth without loss. According to the guerrillas, the Japanese believed that the Americans had escaped from Davao in order to round up guerrillas for an assault on the prison camp itself. The Japanese garrison had been hastily reinforced with the arrival of an extra 200 troops.

'Once in touch with the guerrillas, our main problem was one of physical travel through the unexplored jungles and rough terrain of Mindanao, in an effort to get to where we wanted to go,' wrote McCoy. 'No longer were we on a starvation diet. For instance, I note from my journal that on one morning after we reached the guerrillas we had a breakfast of rice, soft-boiled eggs, vegetables and coffee, all supplied by the Filipinos. On another morning we luxuriated over a menu containing eggs, cottage cheese, carabao meat and coffee.' McCoy was struck by how much food was available. 'This was a decided contrast to our unchanging prison breakfasts of the hated lugao, a concoction of rice and water,'[32] he wrote.

And so the journey continued through trackless and largely unexplored jungle on Mindanao. The Americans faced many perils and discomforts, and they would not have made it without the assistance and supplies given so freely by the Filipino guerrillas. Mellnik's hand gave him considerable pain, and at one point Dobervich became quite ill. 'We thought he had a recurring attack of malaria, although his symptoms were slightly atypical,' wrote McCoy. 'After several days on quinine, during which he showed no change for the better, I switched him to aspirins, of which we had hoarded a small store from our Red Cross boxes. He was soon better.'

Some of the journey was completed in a native banca, a type of riverboat, during which they passed through the territory of the Atas, a primitive tribe who lived in tree houses. 'These natives use spears and poisoned arrows as weapons, but they seemed friendly to us,' wrote McCoy.

Any immersion in water resulted in a plague of fat black leeches stuck all over their bodies. 'One of the worst parts of our journey led through dense jungle in which we waded through water as deep as our armpits,' wrote McCoy. 'This jungle was infested with leeches which traveled with a jackknife motion through the water, and which attached themselves to our flesh by the score, despite our efforts to keep them off. We wore our socks outside our trousers, and then used improvised leggings, but somehow the leeches got through.' Horrified, the Americans stripped off after each immersion and with trembling fingers attempted to lever the bloodsuckers off of each other's bodies. 'Once attached to the skin, they would suck out blood and puff themselves out like a balloon. The only way to remove them was to apply fire or tobacco.'

On one occasion the escapees nearly ran into 200 Japanese infantry who were combing the forest for them, covered by five fighter planes that were wheeling high above and acting as spotters for the ground searchers below. The escapers came upon cloven-hoofed tracks in the jungle mulch caused by the peculiar Japanese boots that separated the big toe from the other toes. They were very lucky not to have been recaptured on this occasion.

McCoy's story comes to an abrupt end at this point, but somehow they made it to the coast and onto a Filipino fishing launch. The Japanese were never far away, and the fear of recapture was a constant worry for all of the Americans. One morning they were hidden on the boat when the dawn revealed that they were inadvertently trailing two armed and fast Japanese coastal patrol boats. Knowing that to veer suddenly away would likely cause the Japanese to become suspicious and investigate, the Filipino crew continued to boldly follow the Japanese craft until the enemy vessels mercifully turned to port for a run-in to a local harbour. The Filipino fishing boat got away from the area as fast as possible with the Americans hardly daring to breathe.

Later – and the story is incomplete here – Filipino guerrillas managed to smuggle the American escapees out of Mindanao and onto an American submarine. The men were taken in several groups to Australia to recover from their ordeal and thence to the United States for further rehabilitation. The escape of ten men, eight of them American service personnel, from the clutches of the Japanese was a major propaganda coup for the Allies. What the escapees had to say about conditions on the Bataan Death March and inside the Philippine POW camps shocked America, and further hardened its resolve to defeat Japan. 'We believe the facts as presented give a fair picture of the enemy we face in the Pacific,'[33] commented McCoy in 1944. President Roosevelt personally reviewed all of the reports produced by the brave Davao escapers and agreed wholeheartedly with McCoy.

Despite getting lost in the jungle, the Americans thought very highly of their two convicted murderer guides Benigno de la Cruz and Victorio Jumarung. They later appealed to exiled Philippine President Manuel Quezon for their pardon, which he granted.

For the eight American personnel who had made it to freedom, their only thought was getting back into the war and getting some revenge for their own ordeals, and for the deaths of their comrades. 'We were fighting men once more!' wrote William Dyess, and he really was speaking for every member of the 'Davao Eight'.

Chapter 6

Three Thousand Miles to Freedom

His Majesty the Emperor has been deeply anxious about all prisoners of war

Lieutenant Colonel Y. Nagatomo,
Thanbyuzayat Camp, Burma, 28 October 1942

Private Roy Pagani tore along a jungle trail as though the Hounds of Hell were at his heels. The heat was stifling and sweat poured down his face from the exertion. The vegetation was alive with the chirruping and squawking of insects and birds. Mosquitos buzzed around his head as he panted and hurried on. The Japanese would not be far behind and capture was not an option. He was dressed like a Burmese native, a turban wrapped around his head, his feet bare and filthy. A small bag worn across his shoulder contained a meagre supply of food and water. Thus clad and supplied the young British soldier determined to walk a thousand miles to India.

Roy Pagani was born in Fulham, London, in July 1915 to an English father and a French mother. His parents split when he was only four years old, and he was subsequently educated at an all-boys convent school. Pagani left school at thirteen to look for work. In July 1933, at the age of eighteen, Pagani passed an army recruiting office on his bicycle and in a spur of the moment decision he dismounted, leaned his bike against a wall and stepped inside. 'He went in and said that he wanted to join, but at five feet, five inches he was an inch shy of the required height,' recalled his wartime friend and fellow prisoner, Sergeant John Boyd of the US Army Air Corps. 'The recruiting sergeant said that if he could stretch a little higher. Pagani raised his heels a bit and was instantly accepted.'[1] Pagani served in India between 1934 and 1937 before returning to the UK where he married in 1939, shortly before the outbreak of hostilities.

In October 1939 Pagani went over to France with the British Expeditionary Force. Because he spoke fluent French he found valuable work as an interpreter. On 10 May 1940 the Germans unleashed their blitzkrieg into France and the Low Countries, and for three weeks Pagani retreated towards salvation at Dunkirk with his unit, eventually reaching the safety of Dover on 1 June. After rest and retraining Pagani joined the elite Reconnaissance Corps.

The motto of the Reconnaissance Corps was 'Only The Enemy In Front', which was an accurate description of its operational role of gathering tactical intelligence on the battlefield. 'Recce' Corps battalions would probe ahead of advancing British infantry divisions and also screen the flanks of an advance. The work was necessarily extremely dangerous and it required a special sort of soldier – one who was both intelligent and aggressive. Only the most promising soldiers were recruited for the Recce Corps from the infantry battalions, the Corps being considered an elite formation similar in both ethos and selection to other recently created British units such as The Parachute Regiment and The Special Air Service. Before he could join, a soldier had to undertake a five-week course with technical units to determine whether he would be a driver, wireless operator or a mechanic. Most Recce Corps soldiers were highly trained in two of these skills, in addition to their training as infantrymen.

The nature of the role meant that the Recce Corps regiments were highly mobile, being equipped with lorries, Universal (Bren) Gun Carriers and Humber Light Reconnaissance Cars. Each Recce Corps regiment had an HQ Squadron which included anti-tank, signals and mortar troops, and three reconnaissance squadrons that each consisted of three scout troops and an assault troop.[2]

The assault troop was heavy infantry that could be rushed to any point in lorries to overcome enemy resistance that was encountered by any of the lightly armed scout troops.

Pagani joined 18th Reconnaissance Battalion that sailed for Egypt in October 1941 aboard the 30-year-old Canadian liner *Empress of Asia*. In the end, the battalion was to spend three long months at sea, leaving the men exhausted and unfit. When Japan launched its assault on Malaya on 8 December 1941 the unit was ordered with the rest of 18th (East Anglian) Infantry Division to sail to Singapore and reinforce the garrison there.

The unit's title revealed its origins: 18 Reconnaissance Battalion (The Loyals). Originally, Pagani's unit had been the 5th Battalion, The Loyal Regiment (North Yorkshire). It was a first-line Territorial Army unit from Bolton that was converted into a Reconnaissance Corps battalion on 26 April 1941.

Pagani and his comrades very nearly did not make it to Singapore. The *Empress of Asia* was attacked near Singapore by nine Japanese dive-bombers on 5 February 1942. A primary cause for the sinking of the ship was its large contingent of Irish stokers from the Free State. Whenever the ship came under attack they immediately left their stations and went to the boat deck, claiming that as citizens of a neutral country they were entitled not to participate in any action. Naturally, the big liner immediately lost power and became a juicy target for Japanese aircraft as she fell behind the rest of the convoy. Army volunteers quickly replaced most of the mutinous stokers but they could not keep up steam and the ship fell further behind. She was repeatedly struck by bombs and caught fire. 'Soon several fires had started. The worst was amidships which effectively cut her in two, preventing people from getting from one end to the other.'[3] The ship was extensively damaged and burning out of control. 'Eventually her master dropped anchor on a sandbank just outside the harbour and gave the order to abandon ship.'[4] Commander Wilfred Harrington of HMAS *Yarra* bravely manoeuvred his corvette along the *Empress*'s stern and took off 1,804 survivors. Only sixteen men died on the ship, but all of the military stores and equipment aboard the liner were destroyed by fire.

As an aside to Pagani's story, the *Empress of Asia*'s chief mate, Canadian Leonard Johnson, shared Pagani's later determination to avoid capture at all costs. Johnson was never actually imprisoned by the Japanese – he managed to stay a few days ahead of their advance. He gathered together forty of his crew and they managed to get to Sumatra using inter-state steamers. From there, Johnson and his men hiked over 100 miles across the island to catch a ferry to Java. From the Javan capital, Batavia, Johnson and his men commandeered a flat-bottomed riverboat and managed to steam all the way to Freemantle in Australia. For this extraordinary feat Johnson received an OBE.

Having lost all of its transport, weapons and kit 18 Reconnaissance Battalion required refitting before it could be used against the Japanese. Unfortunately, there was neither the time nor the equipment available to re-equip the unit for its original role so along with the rest of 18th (East Anglian) Division it was thrown into the defence of Singapore as dismounted infantry. It would only fight for a few days before General Percival surrendered the colony.

The primary use for 18 Reconnaissance Battalion occurred on 10–11 February, just a few days before the capitulation. Percival recognised that it was strategically vital to recapture the village of Bukit Timah and the hill that stands behind it. Bukit Timah was located just north of the Singapore City defensive perimeter and nearby was a racecourse that was acting as one of the main supply depots for the British garrison. If the Japanese captured the ammunition, food and fuel dumps Percival's ability to hold Singapore would have been seriously compromised.

18 Reconnaissance formed part of a hastily assembled scratch brigade along with the 4th Battalion, The Royal Norfolk Regiment and the 1/5th Battalion, Sherwood Foresters. Under the command of Lieutenant Colonel Lionel Thomas, the battlegroup was christened 'Tomforce'. On 10 February, 18 Reconnaissance advanced straight up the duel carriageway towards Bukit Timah with the other battalions on the flanks. The Norfolks managed to take the hill and hold it for a short time, while 18 Reconnaissance, with a few scrounged Bren gun carriers, had a hard fight for Bukit Timah railway station. However, the appearance of Japanese tanks meant that Tomforce was forced to withdraw on 11 February and Bukit Timah was lost to the Japanese. The brigade pulled back under heavy attack to Singapore's Adam Road and dug in. Less

than four days later the British defence of Singapore came to an abrupt end.

Corporal Pagani approached his commanding officer, Major D.R. Lullineux, on the evening of the 15 February with a request. Pagani told him that he was unable to comply with the surrender order and that he wanted permission to try and escape from Singapore. Lullineux readily gave Pagani his permission and also wished him good luck, for the odds of getting away from the island were extremely slim. Practically every vessel that had attempted to run the Japanese blockade south to Java and Australia had been intercepted and sunk and it seemed unlikely that a soldier on his own would get very far. But Pagani's determination was very much in the spirit of the Recce Corps, and to be expected of an elite soldier.

Pagani made his way down to the bomb-ravaged and burning docks, where hours earlier, amid scenes of horrendous chaos, death and desperation, the last ships had tried to leave crowded with soldiers and civilians united in their desire to escape from the brutal Japanese. Pagani found plenty of abandoned motor launches still tied up alongside the harbour wall. Military equipment was scattered all around, with rifles, steel helmets and webbing mixed up with civilian suitcases on the quay. Dense black smoke continued to pour from the bombed warehouses and abandoned trucks and cars. Dead bodies lay everywhere, many cut down by shrapnel from Japanese bombs and artillery shells. Pagani, in rising desperation, furiously tried to start the engines on several of the launches, but to no avail. Night began to fall. Then he spotted a 15-foot sampan loaded with fish dung and jumped aboard her. The native craft had a rudder and a small sail, but no engine. 'As Singapore burned the sampan slowly moved across the calm water. Pagani slumped over the tiller and peered into the darkness, struggling to stay awake.'[5] Exhaustion threatened to overcome Pagani at any minute. 'He realised that if he were to keep the boat on course he would have to go ashore and get some rest. He landed, secured the little boat and promptly fell asleep.'[6]

On the evening of 16 February Pagani awoke refreshed and ready to continue his journey south. He realised that his best chance of staying free was to island hop down the chain of small islands that are located below Singapore, travelling by night to avoid detection by roving Japanese naval vessels and aircraft. Before dawn on 17 February Pagani landed again. He made contact with some friendly Malays who fed him and watched his boat while he gained some much-needed sleep. In the evening Pagani took to the dark water again and sailed south to another jungle-covered island where he made contact with a local Chinese merchant, who kindly provided him with rations and also watched over him while he rested.

Before dawn on 19 February an exhausted Pagani beached his sampan on Moro Island where he discovered to his amazement a small party of British soldiers. The soldiers had been sent to these outlying islands to assist fugitives who were escaping from Singapore, part of a chain of British troops who guarded caches of supplies on several lonely islands. The idea was to move fugitives down the island chain to Sumatra in the Netherlands East Indies (NEI) (now Indonesia) where the Japanese had not yet landed. The troops had been told to linger for several days following the surrender of Singapore, help as many fugitives as they could, and when they felt sure that no-one else was going to make it, pack up and make their way to Sumatra. 'The British soldiers advised Ras to go to Sumatra because the chances of surviving an open ocean voyage to Australia in such a small boat were slim.'[7] Pagani (known as Ras) sensibly agreed with them and after taking some provisions he set off once again south.

'During the second night he was caught in a terrible storm. He lowered the sail and secured the boat. But as the storm intensified waves repeatedly broke against the side of the boat.' Pagani did not expect to survive the night. 'Fearing he would be thrown into the sea, Ras lay flat across the boat and clung to the gunwhales.'[8] For hours he was tossed about like a cork on the roiling ocean, and he prayed aloud for salvation as the wind howled and salt spray lashed his face. But as suddenly as it had begun, the storm abated just before dawn. Pagani had survived – whether by good fortune or the hand of God he could not say. Peering into the growing light Pagani espied low-lying land about a mile distant. He hoisted sail and tacked the sampan into the mouth of a wide brown river.

'After creeping up the river for several hours he finally saw a small group of men. They waved that he should come ashore. They were British soldiers; another link in the escape chain he had discovered on Moro Island. He had made it to Sumatra ...'[9]

Pagani, along with thousands of other soldiers and civilians, crossed Sumatra to the east coast port of Padang where evacuation ships were arriving to take them to India. For nearly two weeks Pagani waited in Padang for his turn to board an evacuation transport as the Japanese launched their invasion of Sumatra and headed for the port.

The defence of the NEI rested primarily upon the defence of Java, a big island next to Sumatra, and the administrative capital of the archipelago. A mixed force of 30,000 British, Dutch, Australian and American troops defended Java, and an unreliable locally raised Home Guard consisting of 40,000 Indonesians backed up the regulars. Allied air power was extremely limited as it was throughout the rest of Asia, although a mixed Allied naval force of eight cruisers and sixteen destroyers in various states of repair or refit were available to launch a pre-emptive strike against the Japanese invasion force when it struck the NEI in late February 1942.

The naval option appeared to be the best solution for preventing the Japanese from obtaining a firm foothold in the NEI, and so on 27 February a combined British-American-Dutch-Australian squadron attempted to intercept the Imperial Japanese Navy's eastern invasion convoy. The attempt went disastrously wrong when the Allied force instead clashed with a powerful covering group of battleships and heavy cruisers. Several Allied warships, including two Dutch cruisers, were lost in what was subsequently named the Battle of the Java Sea. What was left of the Allied naval force scattered, most of its units heading for safety and refit in Australia. Two heavy cruisers, the Australian HMAS *Perth* and the American USS *Houston*, made for Batavia in Java but were both sunk when they stumbled into and then attacked the Japanese western invasion convoy, heavily protected by another powerful group of warships. With the failure of the Allied combined naval operation to prevent the Japanese from landing, the defence of Java was already effectively over before a single Japanese infantryman had stepped ashore.

In a few days of confused battles on Java and Sumatra the Allied forces were roundly defeated. Major General Hervey Sitwell, officer commanding British forces on Java, surrendered on 12 March to Lieutenant General Maruyama of 2nd Imperial Guards Division. Sitwell was captured alongside Brigadier Arthur Blackburn, VC, who had commanded Australian troops that were known collectively as 'Black Force', and Brigadier S.H. Pearson, commanding the British 16th Anti-Aircraft Brigade. No respecters of rank, General Sitwell, as we learned in Chapter 1, received his first beating at the hands of his captors only eight days after capture, after he had refused to divulge military secrets, behaviour that was expressly forbidden under the terms of the Geneva Convention.

While General Sitwell was enduring torture and abuse at the hands of the Japanese, Corporal Pagani was as determined as he had been at the fall of Singapore to escape from the rapidly approaching Japanese. To this end, on 15 March, with Japanese infantry closing in on Padang, Pagani joined up with a motley assortment of beached British sailors off the sunken battleship HMS *Prince of Wales* and together they located a small steam tug that was tied up and apparently abandoned in the harbour. Though not an ideal craft with which to attempt to cross the Bay of Bengal, Pagani and his comrades were nonetheless prepared to at least try.

Two days later, with the tug full of provisions, they steamed across the harbour towards the open sea. But disaster struck. The Japanese had taken Padang moments before and soldiers fired a machine gun across the tug's bows, ordering it in no uncertain terms to return to the docks. Pagani's luck had finally run out and he now found himself a prisoner of the Japanese. Considering his tremendous efforts to remain free since the surrender of Singapore, this was a bitter disappointment.

Five hundred British soldiers and sailors, along with around 700 Australian and Dutch servicemen, were taken prisoner in Padang and herded into a local barracks. The Japanese issued no rations, and only men who still had some cash ate as the Japanese forced the prisoners to pay for food from a Chinese contractor. After a few days, the Japanese organised the POWs into groups that consisted of 20 officers and 480 other ranks. These groups were then sub-divided into four companies and were sent by train

100 miles north to Fort Dekok. From there, Pagani and the other prisoners went to the small port of Belawan Deli and were loaded onto a rusty transport ship for the short journey to Mengui, Burma. They were destined to become slave labourers on one of the most ambitious and deadly military engineering projects undertaken during the war – the infamous Burma-Thailand Railway.

Known to the POWs as the 'Railway of Death', it was well named. In order to maintain the forces in Burma the Japanese had to bring in all their supplies and troops by sea through the submarine-infested Strait of Malacca and the Andaman Sea. They therefore devised a plan to construct a railway from Thailand to Burma through territory so impenetrable that the British had abandoned a similar scheme just before the war after surveyors stated that it could not be done. The difference between the British and the Japanese was that the latter were prepared to sacrifice tens of thousands of lives in order to make the project a reality.

The Japanese plan involved connecting Ban Pong in Thailand with Thanyuzayat in Burma through the Three Pagodas Pass, a distance of 258 miles. Construction began at both ends in late June 1942 and to build the railway the Japanese assembled a total of 330,000 labourers, including 61,000 Allied POWs. Most of the tracks and sleepers were from dismantled railways in Malaya and the Netherlands East Indies.

The railway was completed on 17 October 1943 when the two lines met just south of Three Pagodas Pass at a town called Konkuita in Kanchanaburi Province, Thailand. The railway was built at enormous human cost – 90,000 Asian labourers died along with 16,000 Allied POWs (including 3,585 British). One of the worst episodes occurred at Hellfire Pass, where a huge labour force of Allied POWs was forced to construct a deep cutting through solid rock in the Tenasserim Hills. The Japanese beat sixty-nine POWs to death in six weeks, and dozens more died from disease and starvation.[10] Ironically, all the death and effort was ultimately for nothing as no sooner had the railway been completed than several of the railway bridges, most famously Bridge 277 or 'The Bridge on the River Kwai', were destroyed by Allied aircraft. After the war the British surveyed the Railway of Death and found that it was of such poor construction that it could not support commercial traffic.

Roy Pagani's transport ship, part of a small coastal convoy, arrived at Mergui on 25 May 1942. For several months the POWs were kept in a camp where they endeavoured to do as little as possible in the enervating climate until on 21 October they were boarded onto barges and shipped downriver to the coast. Pagani and his comrades soon arrived at the Burmese coastal port of Moulmein. The Japanese marched the prisoners to Moulmein Station and the following day a train took them thirty miles to Thanbyuzayat, the site of the main junction for the Burma-Thailand Railway. Pagani and the others were expected to construct the junction at Konkuita in Kanchanaburi Province, Thailand, and would be based at the infamous Thanbyuzayat Camp (also known as 18KM Camp) for the duration.

'The brutal 18KM prison camp was under the command of a Japanese Colonel Nagitomo [Lieutenant Colonel Y. Nagatomo]. The day after the prisoners arrived at 18KM camp, Nagitomo made a speech that was a strange mixture of friendliness and threats.' In a scene that inspired a famous moment in the film *The Bridge on the River Kwai*, the ragged and exhausted Allied prisoners were drawn up into ranks on a dusty parade ground before the stiff and formal Japanese camp staff. The diminutive Colonel Nagatomo strutted out onto a wooden dais, one hand holding his samurai sword, where he made a speech of 'welcome' (reproduced in full in 'Appendix C', it neatly encapsulates the Japanese military mind at the time and its attitude to Allied POWs). He berated the prisoners over the fact that Emperor Hirohito had decided to spare them. 'The Imperial Thoughts are unestimable [sic] and the Imperial Favours are infinite,' declared Nagatomo, 'and as such, you should weep with gratitude at the greatness of them.'[11]

In a later part of his speech he delineated the regulations concerning escape. 'The rules of escape shall naturally be severe', warned Nagatomo. 'If there is a man here who has at least 1% of a chance of escape, we shall make him face the extreme penalty.' The prisoners were informed of their hopeless geographic situation with relish. 'If there is one foolish man who is trying to escape, he shall see big jungles toward the East which are impossible for communication,' said Nagatomo. 'Towards the West he should see boundless ocean and, above all, in the main points of North, South, our Nippon Armies are guarding.'

Corporal Pagani soon realised that every day that he spent as a slave labourer on the railway would sap his strength and destroy his health, meaning that escape would become more and more of a remote idea. He therefore quickly formulated two individual escape plans. The first plan involved heading west to the Bay of Bengal, a distance of ten miles from the camp. Once at the coast Pagani would search for and steal a boat and then tack along the Burmese coast to India. If he was unable to find a boat, Pagani's second plan involved a walk of not less than 1,000 miles to freedom. He would double back to Moulmein and then head north overland through Burma to India. His epic trek would take him through some of the toughest country on earth where tropical diseases abounded, and he could not speak the languages of the natives upon whom he would have to rely for food and water during his journey. 'Ras had, however, prepared himself for this journey. He was now as brown as a native and his feet were hard for the trip (to pass as a native he would have to travel without shoes). He had a full brownish-red beard. He looked like a Burmese native, and the Japanese would be looking for an Englishman.'[12]

Realising that he did not have a moment to lose, Pagani determined to escape from the camp just two days after having formulated his plans. When dawn broke on escape day Pagani was already up and he quickly breakfasted on the small bowl of rice gruel that the Japanese deemed sufficient nutrition for slaves before attending the obligatory morning *tenko* or roll call.

The Japanese routinely beat up any prisoners who reported for sick call who looked like they were still able to work. After a short bashing the offending prisoner was handed a changkul, a native hoe, and ordered out unescorted to join a working party some distance beyond the camp's main gate. The Japanese did not bother to escort individual prisoners because they believed escape was impossible.

Pagani duly reported sick. He was beaten, handed a changkul and ordered to join a working party outside the camp. When he was about 100 yards beyond the main gate, and with his changkul across his shoulder, he simply stepped off the track and into the dark jungle. He knew that the Japanese would not miss him until evening *tenko*, and they would probably not start looking for him until the following morning.

Moving quickly, Pagani reached the coast in four hours. But search though he did, he failed to locate a boat. As he was only ten miles from the camp Pagani realised that he could not waste much more time searching and he fell back onto his Plan B – walking to India. He immediately set off in a northeasterly direction until he reached the railway line and followed this north towards Moulmein.

Pagani reached Thanbyuzayat, a small village near Moulmein later that afternoon. He was still only twenty-five miles from the camp, but he could not afford to wait until nightfall before passing through the village and on to Moulmein. Quickly donning an Indian pagri, a kind of turban commonly worn by Indian labourers in the region, he stooped and rubbed dirt into his legs and then onto his face in an effort to further disguise his European features. Once suitably filthy Pagani boldly set off down the village's main street.

As Pagani walked down the street some of the locals cast him suspicious glances. Suddenly, a five-man Japanese patrol appeared and began to saunter towards him. 'He overcame the natural instinct to run and instead casually walked toward a house to urinate,' recalled Pagani's friend Sergeant John Boyd. 'In India it was common for men to simply squat in public to urinate. Since his survival depended on passing as a native Ras followed the local custom.'[13] Pagani's ruse worked perfectly and the Japanese soldiers strolled by, barely casting him a glance. Shortly after Pagani ducked behind the curtain of an empty shop stall and fell into an exhausted sleep.

He awoke after sundown. He immediately set off for the railway line and once he had located it followed the metal rails towards Moulmein. He walked all night. As the first light of dawn began to spread across the horizon Pagani came to a small shack set on the edge of rice paddy fields. An Indian emerged and after a nervous conversation he permitted Pagani to rest inside the hut until darkness fell once again that evening.

Pagani again walked all through the night until, exhausted, he happened upon another wooden hut at dawn. The Indian who emerged from inside, Muhammad Esoof, told Pagani that he had served in the Indian Army, and he was clearly very pro-British. Esoof warned Pagani against entering the city of Moulmein, which was swarming with Japanese troops. Instead, Esoof advised Pagani to swim across the Salween River and bypass Moulmein and its hostile garrison. Esoof then added that his brother was a fisherman and had a boat. Eventually it was agreed that Esoof's brother would ferry Pagani across the Salween.

The journey took about an hour. Esoof and his brother dropped Pagani off on the north bank and they waved a cheerful farewell. Then Pagani once more struck out along the railway line beyond Moulmein. For two days he trekked and eventually the wild jungle gave way to more orderly plantation. Veering off the railway line, Pagani crept through the trees until he discovered several well-kept buildings. 'He watched the property and soon discovered that the people who lived in the houses were not Burmese,' wrote Sergeant Boyd. 'The place had an unmistakable feel of prosperity. He surmised that the people had prospered under the British and most likely did not look upon the Japanese with good favour.'[14]

Pagani decided to take a risk and knock on the front door of the main residence. A surprised servant opened the door and instructed that Pagani should wait. The door was re-opened and a young, well-dressed woman speaking perfect English politely invited the dirty and smelly Pagani into her elegant home. The woman explained that this was the home of her father, Po Thin, a wealthy Karen timber merchant. The Karens are a fiercely independent Burmese hill people. When Pagani was introduced to Po Thin the young soldier told the story of his many attempts to evade capture since Singapore and of his imprisonment on the railway. In a supreme irony, Pagani learned that Po Thin's company was producing the timber that the Japanese were using to construct the Railway of Death. Po Thin was impressed with Pagani's story, and he was also very well connected with the Karen resistance movement up in the nearby hills. He told Pagani that he wanted to help him reach Allied lines, and that the best move he could make was to go up into the Karen Hills where an eccentric British major was busy training guerrillas to fight the

Japanese. 'What Po Thin didn't tell Ras was that he had already sent a runner to the major to inform him of the Englishman's arrival and seek his advice.'[15]

The runner soon returned with instructions from the Major ordering Pagani to be brought to his camp immediately. Pagani was concealed in a refuse truck and smuggled past a Japanese checkpoint by Po Thin's loyal men. After a trek on foot Pagani's small party was met by a cart and a driver named Saw Willie Saw for the final journey to the Karen's camp.

Willie and Pagani eventually reached the small village of Molopa high in the scrub-covered Karen Hills after several hours. The village contained an extraordinary mixture of soldiers and civilians. Mixed in with the Karen guerrillas were Indians and even Gurkhas who had become separated from their units during the Japanese invasion of Burma and had joined the Karens. Pagani met the mysterious Major who was known to his native troops as 'Grandfather Longlegs'. Pagani did not recognise the tall native who walked towards him smiling until he announced cheerfully 'Hello old chap, how are you?' in clipped public school English. Beneath the native clothing was an Englishman, and a rather extraordinary Englishman at that.

'It was a heart warming moment,' recalled Sergeant Boyd. 'The man introduced himself as Major Hugh Seagrim. He grasped Ras' hand and in a voice choked with emotion kept telling him how glad that he was that he had come. After the trials and fears Ras had experienced during the past few months he felt his eyes fill with tears at this greeting.'[16]

33-year-old Hugh Seagrim had been born in Ashmansworth, Hampshire, and after Sandhurst had joined the 19th Hyderabad Regiment in India. Seconded to the 20th Burma Rifles with the temporary rank of major, Seagrim, an expert linguist, had joined Force 136 and had been tasked with training the loyal Karens to fight the Japanese. Force 136 was the Far Eastern arm of Special Operations Executive, Churchill's covert force raised in 1940 to carry out sabotage against the enemy.

Major Seagrim was 6 feet 4 inches tall, hence his affectionate nickname from the Karens, who adored the eccentric Englishman. His sabotage activities had already earned Seagrim a DSO and an MBE. Pagani and Seagrim both realised that the Japanese would be searching for their missing prisoner. Seagrim decided that henceforth Pagani would be known as 'Corporal Ras', hoping that if he was recaptured the Japanese would not link him with their missing Corporal Roy Pagani. Escape usually brought with it the death penalty under Japanese military law, and the Japanese were also not keen for their mistreatment of Allied POWs slaving on the Railway of Death to become widely known. If recaptured and correctly identified by the *Kempeitai*, the Japanese Military Police, Pagani would probably have been beheaded or shot.

Pagani and Seagrim formed a close bond over the ten days that they spent in each other's company. Seagrim delighted in tutoring Pagani on the hill tribes of Burma, and he respected the corporal for his bravery and resolution in escaping from the Japanese. For his part, Pagani said that Major Seagrim was the finest officer that he had had the pleasure to encounter during the war.

Seagrim made Pagani his commander for his southern area of operations – the young corporal had become a guerrilla leader by chance. 'Pagani and his partisans, operating from Kadaingti on the Yunzalin River, made many raids on enemy patrols, villages and convoys, successfully destroying much transport,' reads an official report dating from 1946.

On 9 April 1943 Pagani was reluctantly sent by Seagrim on a mission to contact Allied forces in the Prome region to send word on his activities through to higher command headquarters. Seagrim would furnish Pagani with Karen guides, as well as a letter for his superiors. 'They spent their final day together making preparations for Ras's journey,' wrote Boyd. 'Early the next morning Ras said good-bye to Seagrim and started for Pyagawpu to collect a gun from the stockpile of weapons that Seagrim and the Karen guerrillas had cached.'[17]

It was a bittersweet parting between Pagani and Seagrim – two Englishmen who were far from home in a strange and dangerous land. As he neared the jungle Pagani looked back and saw Seagrim. He suddenly seemed like a very lonely figure and at that moment Ras almost regretted his enthusiasm for his journey. But then Seagrim raised his hand in a farewell salute. Ras returned the salute and continued on through the clearing. The next time the two men would encounter each other would be under very different circumstances.

After leaving Seagrim, Corporal Pagani travelled north with his bodyguard, Lance Corporal Mura and eight of Seagrim's armed guerrillas. They reached Pyagawpu without incident and Ras and Mura were taken to a local Baptist minister's house where Seagrim's weapons cache was located and Pagani armed himself with a gun and ammunition. Pagani's intended destination was a group of friendly Karen villages in a coastal area of Burma called the Arakan Yomas. In order to reach the Karen he would have to cross Burmese territory, including the mighty Irrawaddy River. Pagani calculated that reaching the river would take a minimum of six days on foot. He discharged his Karen guards and sent them back to Major Seagrim, only retaining as his guide Lance Corporal Mura.

The next day Mura was captured following a fight with hostile Burmese, during which Pagani only just managed to escape. Alone once again, Pagani, after resting in a Buddhist temple, continued on towards the Irrawaddy. Two days later he accepted food and a place to rest from a monk at a Burmese pagoda. Hearing aircraft, Pagani dashed outside to see a formation of USAAF B-25 Mitchell bombers on their way to attack the city of Prome, 150 miles north of Rangoon. At this point Pagani had an idea. Realising that he could be recaptured at any moment, he felt that it would be a good idea to completely divorce his identity from the British Army, as the Japanese might still manage to make the link between 'Corporal Ras' and their missing Corporal Pagani. Thinking of his baby son back in England, Terry Ashton Melvin Pagani, he decided to re-invent himself as a shot down American air force officer named 'Lieutenant Terry Ashton Melvin'. He had already destroyed his identity documents and disposed of his army dog tags. It proved to be a wise move, as things later turned out.

After another night's walk, Pagani arrived on the east bank of the Irrawaddy River. Beyond the fast-flowing brown waters lay the Arakan Yomas with its friendly Karen villages. Pagani spent a fruitless few hours searching for a boat until he realised that his only hope of salvation was to swim the river. He was a strong swimmer, but the current was also strong and unpredictable.

Before he climbed into the water, Pagani carefully destroyed the letter that Major Seagrim had given to him to take to army head-quarters that contained details of Pagani's battlefield promotion to sergeant. This done, Pagani stepped into the warm waters and began to strike out for the western bank that he could clearly make out in the moonlight. 'About 150 yards from the bank he was caught in a strong undertow that, coupled with the weight of his gun and ammunition, threatened to pull him under,' wrote Sergeant Boyd. 'He dumped his gun and spare ammunition and floated downstream, but the current pushed him back onto the east bank of the river.'[18]

Exhausted, Pagani was spotted by two Burmese men in a fishing boat, who picked him up. But then a commotion was heard coming from the bank and a crowd of about fifty Burmese, many of them armed with shotguns, ordered the fishermen to hand Pagani over. The escape attempt that had carried Pagani from the Death Railway to the banks of the Irrawaddy was over, for these Burmese wanted to hand him to the Japanese in return for a small finder's fee. Amid much commotion, shouting, pushing and shoving, Pagani was bound with rope and led away. At one point Pagani managed to slip his bonds and he made a wild dash for the nearest jungle, but a bullet in his side ended his last break for freedom. 'Beaten and bloody, Ras thought of his wife and young son and his promise that he would return home,' said Boyd. 'That promise would now be broken. They would never know what happened to him. He had destroyed his identity papers and was now going to die alone, in the darkness near a muddy river in a distant land among a hostile people.'[19]

But Pagani was not killed by the mob of yelling and screaming Burmese – he was too valuable. Instead, hogtied and bleeding, he was transported downriver to a Japanese guard post and handed over. His wound was perfunctorily treated, without anaesthetic, before he was questioned. He told the Japanese that he was a USAAF officer who had been shot down the night before during a raid on Prome.

Transferred to a hospital in Prome, Pagani endured a painful operation on his gunshot wound. The pain was so bad that he even contemplated suicide one night, but the thought of his family prevented him from ending his life. Slowly he started to recover his strength. Once strong enough, the Japanese interrogated him in more detail. 'He explained his native clothing by saying that his uniform had caught fire, and the natives had given him what he was wearing. This story seemed to satisfy the Japanese.'[20]

After six weeks in hospital two Japanese soldiers escorted Pagani to the local railway station where the three of them boarded a train to Rangoon. On arrival at his destination, the New Law Courts Building, Pagani learned that he was to be handed over to the *Kempeitai* for further interrogation. His guts turned to water at the thought of what might happen to him in their charge, for the *Kempeitai* Military Police were renowned for brutality and sadism. It was a reputation that Pagani soon discovered was richly deserved.

Placed in a tiny cell with five other prisoners, and ordered not to talk, Pagani witnessed a different prisoner being dragged from the cell each day and brutally interrogated for a couple of hours. The prisoners' screams and the dreadful sounds of physical violence echoed through the large building. Eventually, it was Pagani's turn. He was dragged into a room that contained two Japanese NCOs, each armed with a bamboo cane. One asked the questions, while the other one beat Pagani mercilessly between questions. Pagani stuck to his cover story of being a downed American airman.

Next, Pagani was dragged into a second room where two more interrogators were waiting for him. One of the interrogators was a junior officer, and in between questions this officer would beat Pagani with the back of an unsheathed samurai sword. Sometimes he would level a cocked pistol at Pagani's head and dry fire it. And later during the interrogation the Japanese officer took to swinging his sword at Pagani's exposed neck and stopping the razor-sharp blade only a hair's breadth from his skin. Pagani later learned how lucky he had been, as this particular *Kempeitai* officer had actually beheaded some of the other prisoners when he had failed to stop his cut at the last moment. Finally, Pagani was bundled into a third room where he was tied to a flat surface with his head positioned beneath a dripping tap. After a while each drip of water that hit his forehead felt like a hammer. At some point the questions and the agony abruptly ceased and Pagani was dragged back to his grimy cell to nurse his wounds and contemplate his future.

Pagani expected that this abusive treatment would continue for days, or even weeks, until he either cracked and revealed his true identity, or he died. But surprisingly his endurance paid off, and Pagani found himself cleaned up and sent to Rangoon Jail. He was out of the clutches of the *Kempeitai*, but he now faced an altogether different form of torture in one of the worst POW camps in Asia.

Rangoon Jail, originally built by the British authorities, held nearly 600 Allied prisoners of war by 1944 in appalling conditions. Most of the inmates were British troops who had been captured during the chaotic Allied retreat through Burma, or from Singapore, while many others, including some American B-29 crews, were airmen who had been shot down during bombing and reconnaissance sorties out of RAF bases in India. The Japanese singled out the airmen for particularly tough treatment.

In a response to the famous Doolittle Raid on Tokyo in 1942, the Japanese had hastily sanctioned a new law making air raids on *any* territory controlled by the Japanese a 'war crime'. Shot down Allied airmen were denied prisoner of war status and instead faced military court martials. 'Death shall be the military punishment,' read the Japanese order, and 'shall be by shooting.'[21] The Japanese occasionally allowed for mitigating circumstances, and instead of death airmen were instead sentenced to inhuman imprisonments in circumstances of the greatest cruelty.

'There was one day a truck came in with a group of airmen from some Flying Fortresses that had been shot down and caught fire,' recalled Rifleman Spoors. 'They were all badly burned but were still put into solitary confinement where three died the next day. Our medical officer Colonel [Kenneth] McKenzie saw the Commandant, and got three transferred to our compound and three to another. Only one of them survived, a young lad of about 19 years whose face was burnt, and hands twisted with the burns.'[22]

Spoors recalled the gruesome fate of one badly injured American flyer that the Japanese refused to treat: 'One of the chaps who died in our compound had no eyes at all. His face had been totally burned in the fire, and when he was put into solitary he'd lain unconscious on the earthen floor and his eyes became badly infected with maggots, which just ate his eyeballs away.'[23]

The POWs at Rangoon Jail were fed an inadequate diet of rice that had already been declared unfit for human consumption by the Japanese. The Japanese later changed the staple food to bran, the same wormy bran the Japanese fed to their pigs. Most days the POWs had to make do with a few pumpkins and marrows, and if they were very lucky an Oxo cube-sized lump of meat or a little shark flesh. The prisoners, as well as being riddled with tropical diseases and severely malnourished, also stank as the Japanese restricted them to only two mess tins of water *per week* for washing and shaving purposes. Lacking soap, the prisoners were permanently filthy, which encouraged diseases to spread more quickly through their ranks.

One of the prisoners who ended up inside Rangoon Jail was Corporal Pagani's friend Major Hugh Seagrim. His unit of Karen guerrillas had been steadily worn down in combat, and the Japanese made horrific retaliatory attacks against Karen villages in response to Seagrim's raids and ambushes. Seagrim, a deeply religious man, could not abide the cruelties that were inflicted upon his beloved Karens by the Japanese and on 15 March 1944, in order to spare the civilian population, Seagrim voluntarily surrendered himself to the Japanese after he had received assurances that he would be accorded POW status.

The *Kempeitai* did not torture Seagrim, neither did they abuse him inside Rangoon Jail, as it seems that even the Japanese had some respect for the bravery of 'Grandfather Longlegs'. 'He never seemed to be sick,' recalled an American POW of the illustrious Major. 'He was a very religious man who carried the Bible with him at all times. He would not call the Japanese master. He would not bow to them. He walked tall and straight with his head in the air. Always calm and friendly and doing what he could for his fellow men.'[24]

Seagrim was placed in a cell opposite the Japanese guardhouse. On 2 September 1944 Ras Pagani was a member of a working party that was moving supplies near the guardhouse and main gate. He looked up as a Japanese Army truck drove out of the main gate. In the back of the truck he saw a tall Englishman and seven Karen tribesmen. 'As they started through the breezeway toward the front gate the Englishman saw Pagani, gave him a big smile and waved to him,' recalled fellow POW Sergeant Boyd.

'Pagani returned the wave as the truck pulled out of the prison. It was a few moments before Pagani realised that the Englishman was his beloved Major Hugh Seagrim.'[25]

The Japanese had broken their promise to accord Seagrim and his men POW status. They were instead court-martialled and sentenced to death. Pagani's final encounter with Seagrim saw him witness the Major's departure from Rangoon Jail on 22 September 1944. Seagrim was executed by firing squad later that day alongside his trusted Karen guerrilla fighters. For his extraordinary courage Major Seagrim was posthumously awarded the George Cross in 1946.

In a postscript to Seagrim's story, his brother Derek was posthumously awarded the Victoria Cross for his actions in Tunisia against the Germans, making Hugh and Derek Seagrim the only siblings in British military history to have been awarded Britain's two highest awards for gallantry.

For Pagani and his compatriots, they spent the remainder of the war labouring on the Rangoon Docks. Impressed as unpaid stevedores, the POWs loaded and unloaded cargo ships from early in the morning until late in the evening, stopping only for a short and inadequate lunch that they had to cook themselves and the occasional cigarette break. The work was gruelling, and conducted under a fierce sun or torrential downpours. The prisoners were given every fourth Sunday off as a day of rest:

> The working parties varied in numbers, each one usually with an officer PW in charge. Every man who was able to stand up was made to work. The tasks included docking, bomb disposal, trench digging, making A.A. [Anti-Aircraft] and S/L positions and building bomb shelters. There was one instance of a shelter 18′ deep with 30′ of earth on top including 4 to 5 layers of timber. The hours of work were from 0900 hours to 1330 hours, and from 1430 hours until at the whim of the Japanese guard, he considered they had done enough, which might be 1900 or 2030 hours. Night work was carried out at the docks unloading petrol, rice and bombs.[26]

Occasionally, the prisoners' monotonous routine was broken by a day's labour at the nearby railway station or a truck journey to the old RAF airfield at Mingladon for more back-breaking hard labour. Discipline was enforced through a combination of threats, beatings and outright torture. Failure to bow to Japanese guards usually resulted in a severe thrashing, and the Japanese delighted in punishing entire groups for one prisoner's minor infraction of the camp rules. The sick in the prison hospital were ordered by the Japanese to catch flies and fill two small bottles each day, as the guards delighting in creating yet more physical torment for men who were already extremely ill. Some prisoners inevitably became mentally disturbed. 'I clearly remember a chap called Gilroy from the Inniskillings who had lost a brother in the fighting and another had died of a jungle sore the size of a dinner plate on his thigh,' recalled Rifleman Spoors. 'He cracked up eventually and every morning he would stand by the fence, stick two fingers in his mouth and whistle as loud as he could. He got on our nerves but it must have been worse for the Japs. Eventually they could take it no longer and he was put into solitary confinement where he stayed until our release nearly three years later.'[27]

The death rate in the camp was later determined by a detailed SOE investigation to have been between 20 and 25% of the white prisoners. The causes of death were mainly dysentery, malaria, beriberi, jungle sores and malnutrition, though physical abuse from the guards played an important part as well. There was one outbreak of cholera in the Jail, but the Japanese moved swiftly to eradicate this by inoculating the prisoners. They did this because the guards were also at risk from contracting the disease. The worst example of mass death was the treatment of a group of 500 Dutch POWs who were housed in Rangoon Jail between October 1942 and February 1943. Two hundred and thirteen of them died, mainly of dysentery.[28]

Roy Pagani was liberated on 28 April 1945, along with several hundred survivors, south of the city of Pegu to which the Japanese had forced them to march. The guards had left the POWs to their own devices when it was clear that armoured elements of the British 14th Army were close by.

Pagani's extreme courage, repeated escapes, partisan activities and devotion to duty were rewarded with the Military Medal in February 1947. He had escaped from Japanese-occupied Singapore and escaped from the Burma-Thailand Railway, both times virtually singlehandedly. He had also survived one of the worst camps in the Japanese prison camp system, not to mention his daring guerrilla activities in the Karen Hills. These were amazing, some might say almost miraculous, achievements. Pagani was able to keep the promise that he had made to his wife and young son, and he came home alive unlike 16,000 of his British, Australian, Dutch and American comrades, whose bones today lie in cemeteries the length of the Railway of Death, a grim and moving testimony to the barbarity and madness of the Japanese Army.

Chapter 7

Officially Dead

A single day of solitary confinement can be torture in a cell that had a small window that was too high to look out of. Seven weeks can feel like a lifetime.

Commander Winfield Cunningham, US Navy

Hardly daring to breath, the escapers left their hut and as silently as possible scampered across the hard-pressed dirt towards the low perimeter fence. The men had blackened their faces with soot from the hut stove but they still felt desperately exposed in the semi-darkness of the camp. Several men among them felt a spot itch between their shoulder blades where they expected a bullet at any second. They silently dropped to the dirt beside the fence and lay still for a few seconds, straining their ears like animals for danger. Their breath plumed above their heads in the cold air, but nothing appeared amiss. The camp was quiet, except for the sounds of coughing coming from the freezing huts. Carefully and deliberately, one of the men drew a metal spoon from his jacket pocket and started to scratch at the earth beneath the fence. Like rabbits, the escapers would dig a shallow trench beneath the perimeter wire and then squeeze underneath. Another of the escapers also started digging while two others moved the dirt with their hands and another kept watch.

The sudden sound of footfalls caused the escapers to freeze. Pressing themselves into the earth they watched as a Japanese sentry strolled casually along the perimeter fence towards them, his rifle with its long bayonet twinkling like a baleful star in the poor light. The guard walked closer and closer without seeing the five men who wished with every fibre of their beings that the earth would swallow them. But suddenly the guard halted, about faced and started to walk back the way he had come. The men collectively let out a sigh of relief and went back to their excavations. Within minutes they had scraped away sufficient soil to make a trench and hardly pausing for breath they began to duck under the fence one by one. Once through, they quickly fled into the darkness beyond the camp, aiming to place as much distance between themselves and the camp as humanly possible before sunrise. Among them was the American commander of the legendary last stand on Wake Island in December 1941, the indomitable Commander Winfield Scott Cunningham. The escapers were free of the camp, but very far from real freedom.

Winfield Cunningham never abandoned his will to resist the Japanese. He had led the defence of Wake Island, one of the greatest last stands of the Second World War, endured brutal capture and managed to successfully escape from captivity twice before. Cunningham was imprisoned in some of the most notorious gaols in the Japanese Empire, but his spirit of resistance remained undiminished. Although pronounced 'officially dead' by his own government after Wake, Cunningham was a born survivor and an inspirational leader, whose story has become unjustly overshadowed by some of the other Wake Island heroes. Cunningham, though a prisoner, was undefeated.

In January 1941 the US Navy had begun construction of a permanent base on a tiny Pacific atoll lying between Hawaii and Guam known as Wake Island. It was only two and a half square miles in area, but included a modern airfield. Elements of the 1st Marine Defense Battalion, amounting to 449 officers and men, formed a permanent garrison and were supported by Marine Corps fighter squadron VMF-211 operating twelve outdated Grumman F4F Wildcats. There were also sixty-eight US Navy personnel and 1,150 civilian contractors on the island when the Japanese attack came.

Several 5-inch guns from a defunct First World War American cruiser had been emplaced at strategic points around the atoll, and a variety of anti-aircraft weapons were dug in. The American forces on Wake were placed under a US Navy officer, Commander Cunningham. The Japanese first attempted to reduce Wake on 8 December 1941, the same day their carrier planes devastated the US Pacific Fleet at Pearl Harbor (Wake being on the opposite side of the International Date Line). A bomber offensive was launched that managed to destroy eight of the Wildcats on the ground, a severe blow to the defenders. On the morning of 11 December a Japanese task force that consisted of three light cruisers, six destroyers and a pair of large patrol boats, codenamed the 'South Seas Force', approached the atoll escorting a pair of troop transports loaded with 450 Special Naval Landing Troops. Incredibly, the American defenders were able to send this force packing, sinking the destroyer *Hayate* with 5-inch shells from their dug-in and concealed naval guns, and damaging most of the other ships in a hailstorm of shot and shell. The remaining aircraft of VMF-211 squadron took to the skies and managed to bomb and sink the destroyer *Kisaragi*, forcing the Japanese to place Wake under an aerial siege from land-based medium bombers until a new task force could be constituted.

Deeply humiliated by its unexpected defeat, the Japanese invasion force retreated with its tail between its legs. In the meantime, Admiral Wilson Brown's Task Force 14 had left Pearl Harbor and was steaming towards Wake to relieve the defenders. Brown's force included the aircraft carriers USS *Saratoga* and *Lexington*. The problem was that although the warships were quite swift, they had been forced to match their speed to a slow and elderly fleet oiler, and collectively Brown's task force made slow progress towards Wake. Sadly, when the American task force was within a day of reaching Wake, Vice Admiral William Pye, Acting Commander-in-Chief of what was left of the Pacific Fleet, had second thoughts about risking his carriers in a showdown with a more powerful Japanese fleet known to be converging on Wake for a second invasion attempt, and he ordered Brown to turn about and return his vessels to Pearl Harbor.[1] The American government abandoned the defenders of Wake to their fate, but their refusal to surrender when faced with overwhelming Japanese naval power and to stand and fight to the end proved a huge morale boost to the American public, depressed after the surprise attack on Hawaii.

On 23 December Vice Admiral Sadamichi Kajioka's large invasion fleet arrived off Wake, and after beginning their landings at 2.35am, by the afternoon 1,500 Japanese naval landing troops had come ashore and slowly began to overcome fanatical American resistance, suffering huge casualties in the process.[2] The guns fell silent on Wake on the afternoon of Christmas Eve, 24 December, the day before the British colony of Hong Kong also surrendered after another heroic 'last stand'. Emerging from their defensive positions 1,603 American men, military and civilian, placed themselves into the hands of the Imperial Japanese Navy. Most probably assumed that the worst was now over for them, and their timely capitulation had saved many of their lives when it became clear to their commanders that further resistance was completely futile. American honour had been served in making such a stout defence of the island, and to continue to the 'last man, last round' was not normally a part of the Western military ethos.

American expectations of decent treatment after having fought so gallantly were swiftly dispelled. The Japanese had lost between 700 and 900 naval personnel in their two attempts to take the island, and at least another 1,000 had been wounded. Besides the human cost, Japanese naval pride had been damaged by the loss of two destroyers and twenty aircraft. The Americans had come off much better, with a total of 122 killed, including 49 of the garrison's marines. The Japanese felt that they had been unexpectedly humiliated by this thorn in the side of their otherwise triumphant advance across the Pacific and Southeast Asia, and were in a vengeful mood. Collecting up their prisoners, the Japanese found that the majority were actually American civilians, 1,150 employees of the Morrison-Knudsen Company, who had been sent to Wake to construct an airfield, a seaplane base and a submarine base for the US Navy before the invasion. This only added to the loss of face. The remainder were military prisoners from the US Marine Corps and US Navy.[3]

Although many of the more junior Japanese naval officers were keen to kill the prisoners as soon as possible, Rear Admiral Kajioka, the commander of the Japanese invasion fleet, intervened and forbade any such action. The prisoners were to be kept alive for the time being, and a proper decision would be made higher up the chain of command regarding their ultimate fate. The good news was transmitted by a naval interpreter to the massed ranks of huddled prisoners, filthy, thirsty and exhausted after the fight of their lives: 'The Emperor has gracefully presented you with your lives,' to which some wisecracking American shouted, 'Well, thank the son-of-a-bitch.'[4] Such self-confidence was soon to be knocked out of the prisoners as their ordeal began to unfold.

For three weeks the prisoners loitered around their barracks, until one morning a large Japanese merchant ship hove to in the lagoon. She was the *Nitta Maru*, and her mission was to remove the majority of the men to prison camps in China. The *Nitta Maru* departed from Wake on 12 January 1942, and into her filthy holds were crammed 1,222 American prisoners. A total of 381 civilian contractors and wounded US Marines were left behind on Wake. Two hundred of these were later shipped out, but the remaining ninety-eight were massacred by the Japanese Navy once they had outlived their usefulness.

Before they boarded the *Nitta Maru* the Japanese forced the Americans to 'run the gauntlet'. As Commander Cunningham recalled: 'I had barely picked up one of my bundles [bags of kit] when a Jap struck at my hands and tore it from them. It was like a signal. The double line erupted in hate, and as we ran the gauntlet we were dealt kicks, blows and slaps by men who had no part in our capture.'[5]

Aboard the *Nitta Maru*, food and water was virtually non-existent for the frozen prisoners, huddled together in their own filth in the bowels of the vessel. 'In our long record of semi-starvation as prisoners of war, the twelve days we spent in the voyage from Wake were, at least in my estimation, the worst,'[6] wrote Cunningham. The Japanese physically abused the prisoners, including the officers, relentlessly. 'There was a great deal of slapping,' wrote Cunningham. 'Captain Platt was taken out into the passageway one day and beaten with a club for excessive talking. There was a lack of officer supervision, and the guards took it upon themselves to beat the prisoners.'[7]

The ship arrived in Yokohama in Japan on 20 January, and after a short time in port she set sail for China. The Japanese evidently still felt that they had not been given the chance to take out their frustrations on the American prisoners who had fought them so well, and now away from the gaze of Admiral Kajioka, junior officers plotted a vengeful attack on the defenceless men held down below like animals.

The Japanese guard commander, Lieutenant Toshio Saito, decided to organise a spectacle for both his men and the assembled POWs, an event designed to indicate just how angry the Japanese were over the reverses that they had suffered during the Battle of Wake. Once out at sea the Japanese guards suddenly bundled five of the prisoners topside. The men, all from the Naval Air Station on Wake, were to be tortured to death, in order, said the Japanese, to 'honour their bravery' in the defence of the island. 'You have killed many Japanese soldiers in battle,' announced Saito to the large crowd of American prisoners drawn up on the lurching deck of the ship as Japanese guards, long bayonets fixed to their rifles, stood eyeing the POWs with loathing. Turning to the five bound American victims, Saito continued: 'For what you have done you are now going to be killed for revenge. You are here as representatives of your American soldiers and will be killed. You can now pray to be happy in the next world.' Three Seamen 2nd Class, Theodore Franklin, John Lambert and Roy Gonzales from Patrol Wing 2, and two US Marine Corps NCOs from Marine fighter squadron VMF-211, Master Technical Sergeant Earl Hannum and Technical Sergeant Vincent Bailey, were brutally executed in front of their shocked and horrified comrades in a sickening display of Japanese military sadism.

The bound men were firstly severely beaten and then beheaded with swords by Japanese naval officers.[8] The headless bodies of the American servicemen were then used by gleeful Japanese soldiers and sailors for bayonet practice, until, mutilated beyond recognition, they were dumped over the ship's side like bags of refuse. It is not difficult to imagine the mood among the sickened and appalled American prisoners who had been forced to watch this grisly 'ceremony'. It served as a salutary warning of the kind of treatment that they could expect from their captors from then on.

The *Nitta Maru* finally arrived at Shanghai on 23 January 1942. Hardly had the POWs stepped off the gangway onto Chinese soil when they were subjected to fresh abuse from the Japanese. 'One of the guards, a buck-toothed petty officer wearing glasses, ran up and down the line of prisoners, dealing out blows and kicks for no apparent reason other than to satisfy some sadistic cravings,'[9] recalled Commander Cunningham.

The prisoners' destination was Woosung Camp, located in today's Wusong suburb of Shanghai and home to a naval base. The camp contained a large proportion of American servicemen, mostly members of the 'North China Marines', a group detached to guard the US Consulates in Beijing, Tientsin and Chinwangtao. At that time the surrounding area was mostly flat rice paddies interspersed by small villages and criss-crossed by creeks and canals. One of the few Britons imprisoned at Woosung was Sir Mark Young, the former Governor of Hong Kong who had been captured by the Japanese when the colony surrendered on Christmas Day 1941. After the war Young provided the British government with a detailed report about the camp. 'There were about 1,500 prisoners and conditions, particularly as regards sanitation, were most unsatisfactory,'[10] he recalled. In Shanghai, as elsewhere, the 'Japanese had deliberately chosen run-down and overgrown sites for the internees and did nothing to prepare the facilities for occupation in advance of the foreigners' arrival,'[11] commented Sir Mark.

The wooden barracks huts at Woosung had originally been constructed as a Chinese Nationalist barracks before the war, and they were in a decrepit state when Cunningham and his men arrived. The camp covered about ten acres in total and the Japanese had enclosed the perimeter with an electrified fence. There were seven barracks, each building about seventy feet long and twenty-five feet wide. Next to the back door of each hut there was a squat toilet and wash rack. Inside each barrack block a long corridor ran down the centre, with a series of rooms on each side that contained hard wooden sleeping bays. Into each barracks the Japanese had forced between 200 and 300 men, eighteen or twenty to a room. This form of overcrowding, much favoured by the Japanese authorities, normally encouraged the rapid spread of airborne diseases. The walls of the huts were not insulated so the prisoners nearly froze to death during the harsh Shanghai winters.

The latrines at Woosung were the worst. Chinese coolies using buckets emptied them by hand. In the summer Sir Mark Young recalled that huge clouds of black flies swarmed around the latrines, and then invaded the rest of the camp, landing on food and spreading dysentery. The camp was also infested by rats that scampered under the huts and into the kitchen, adding their excrement to the collective filth.[12]

The situation that the Americans faced in the camp at Woosung made Cunningham reflect long and hard on the decisions that he had taken on Wake. 'I thought of the brave men who had died under my command, and the others who were now mistreated prisoners because I had made the decision to surrender.' The sense of responsibility weighed very heavily upon Cunningham's conscience. 'Over and over I reviewed that decision and others I had made, and I wondered whether different ones might have saved us.'[13] But within Cunningham there also grew a desire to escape from the camp and to fight again – to avenge the humiliation of surrender on Wake.

At Woosung Cunningham shared a room with Lieutenant Commander Columbus Darwin Smith, former commander of the Yangtze River gunboat USS *Wake*. Smith had been recalled to active duty only a few weeks before the attack on Pearl Harbor and ordered to take command of all remaining US Navy installations in Shanghai. Unfortunately, US Navy assets in Shanghai had shrunk to a single small gunboat by then. The *Wake* had been effectively mothballed as a warship and permanently moored astern of the British gunboat HMS *Peterel*.

The *Wake* had only a skeleton crew of fourteen sailors aboard on the morning of 8 December 1941, and eight of these were telegraphists. The vessel had already been rigged with scuttling charges in case the Japanese attempted to capture her. Commander Smith lived ashore in a nearby apartment. At 4am a Japanese boarding party quickly overwhelmed the single American guard and took over the *Wake* without firing a shot, the only occasion during the war when an American warship would be captured without any resistance being offered. Triumphant Japanese marines hauled down the Stars and Stripes and as soon as it was light, photographed themselves with the flag and their rifles, many pumping the air with joy.

Smith arrived shortly after the Japanese had taken the ship and was refused entry to the vessel. Suddenly, from up ahead, firing broke out. HMS *Peterel's* New Zealand skipper, Lieutenant Stephen Polkinghorn, had ordered his small ship's company to make a show of force against the Japanese, whose boarding party had been rudely rebuffed just minutes earlier. It was a desperately uneven fight as the Japanese cruiser *Izumo* bombarded the *Peterel* (which was only armed with Lewis Guns) until the vessel was a smashed and blazing wreck. Several British sailors floated face down in the river, killed by the shelling. As Commander Smith watched, the Royal Navy's last warship in Mainland China rolled over and sank. The Japanese machine-gunned the struggling survivors in the water in one of the first recorded war crimes committed against Allied forces, but some courageous Chinese locals braved the fire to rescue the surviving British sailors and take them to safety in their sampans. Six men were killed, but British naval honour had been saved. Lieutenant Polkinghorn and the survivors were taken prisoner and marched off to Woosung to join the Americans.

It was Commander Smith who first outlined a viable escape plan to Cunningham whilst the two men were imprisoned at Woosung Camp. They were joined in their plotting by a British naval officer, Commander John Woolley, who had been serving as a naval attaché at the British Embassy in Shanghai when the Japanese attacked. Also integral to the plan were Dan Teters, the tough former supervisor of civilian contractors on Wake, and a Chinese teenager named Loo who had been serving aboard the *Wake* as a ship's boy when the vessel was captured.

The escape occurred on the night of 11 March 1942. Avoiding the perimeter guards, the five men carefully dug out a shallow pit beneath the perimeter fence wire and slipped under. Moving silently across country the escapees arrived on a bank of the Yangtze River. Commander Smith's plan was to move down-stream in search of a sampan. The escapees would then steal the boat and ride the tide to Pootung (now Pudong), an area of Shanghai lined with warehouses and godowns opposite the Bund, whose scattered villages were heavily infiltrated by Nationalist Chinese guerrillas. Smith felt sure that the escapees could soon link up with the guerrillas and with their help make their way to Chungking (now Chongqing) and freedom. Smith's plan was ambitious, for the group had not built any contacts with the Chinese Underground before breaking out of Woosung, and the loyalties of the local population could not be counted upon. Loo, the Chinese ship's boy, tried in vain to convince Smith and the others to go west instead of heading for Pootung. 'Strangely enough,' wrote Cunningham, 'we paid no attention to Loo. Convinced that Smith knew what he was doing, we ignored the advice of a man native to the area and took the word of the Occidental who said he knew better.'[14]

The group followed the river to where it joined up with the Huangpu River, the waterway that flows past Shanghai and Pootung. Their search for a sampan was ultimately fruitless, and the group wasted many hours scouring the riverbank. With daylight rapidly approaching Smith knew that they must find some cover, so they broke into a deserted barn and hid. Approaching the farmer for help proved their undoing. The farmer appeared to be sympathetic, but he betrayed them to Chinese government troops loyal to the Quisling Wang Ching-wei regime that the Japanese had established in Nanking. Loo attempted to bargain with the Chinese troops, but all talk of Allied rewards for the safe return of POWs evaporated when heavily armed Japanese soldiers arrived on the scene and surrounded the barn. Smith, Cunningham and the others emerged with their hands above their heads and were herded on board an army truck and taken to Woosung Gaol.

Somewhat surprisingly, the Japanese *Kempeitai* Military Police did not beat and torture the escapees. 'Our interrogators actually seemed to be in good spirits about something,' recalled Cunningham. The reason was that the regular Japanese Army, represented in this instance by the aristocratic Woosung camp commandant, Colonel Yuse, despised the *Kempeitai*. 'The fact that we had escaped from *him* and then been recaptured by *them* filled them with such glee that they were almost grateful to us for the chance to humiliate Yuse.' The *Kempeitai* further eroded Colonel Yuse's already much reduced 'face' by taking Smith and the others back to Woosung Camp and forcing them to recreate their escape for the express purpose of showing Yuse just how bad security at his camp was. The *Kempeitai* also insisted that all of the Woosung prisoners sign a paper agreeing not to try and escape 'or we would be killed', recalled Sergeant Robert Arthur. 'The Wake Island personnel refused to sign ... So we were labelled "dangerous prisoners" and shipped to a prison camp at Kawasaki [Japan].'[15]

On 13 March 1942, Smith, Cunningham, Woolley, Teters and Loo were sent to the infamous *Kempeitai* torture centre that was located in a big white apartment block called Bridge House just north of the Bund over Garden Bridge in Shanghai. There they were to await trial. Again, the escapers were not subjected to any maltreatment, though the cells to which they were confined were very small and overcrowded and they remained locked up for eighteen hours a day. Foreign prisoners at Bridge House were expected to subsist on one pound of bread and two ounces of sugar a day.

The escapees remained at Bridge House for thirty-three long days until they were suddenly marched out and put aboard a truck to Kiangwan Military Prison outside Shanghai on 15 April 1942. On arrival they were strip-searched and then arraigned before a Japanese military court martial.

As discussed earlier, the Japanese did not consider Allied captives to be prisoners of war, instead treating them as 'military prisoners' of the Imperial Army and under army regulations. Therefore, escape, while the duty of a prisoner under agreed international law, was deemed to be 'desertion' by the Japanese authorities and carried with it the severe punishments reserved for Japanese soldiers who attempted it. The Japanese permitted no defence by the prisoners, even though they had prepared one.

Following the show trial, the prisoners were forced into tiny solitary confinement cells for seven weeks and left to await the verdict of the court. Each cell had concrete walls, a wooden floor and no furniture and the prisoners were only permitted thirty-five minutes exercise each day. 'A single day of solitary confinement can be torture in a cell that had a small window that was too high to look out of. Seven weeks can feel like a lifetime,'[16] wrote Cunningham.

In their usual unpredictable manner, the Japanese suddenly announced on 2 June that the men would be tried again. The *Kempeitai* was evidently not satisfied with the first kangaroo court.

This time, Smith, Cunningham and the others tried to raise the question of The Hague and Geneva Conventions that prescribe thirty days solitary confinement as the maximum penalty for escape attempts. The Japanese prosecutor contended that his nation was not bound by any such agreements. This was a half-truth for Japan had signed, though not ratified, the Geneva Convention. Once again the Woosung escapees were tried under the provisions of Japanese military law as deserters from the Imperial Army. Unsurprisingly, all of the defendants were found guilty and sentenced to various terms of imprisonment. Commanders Smith, Cunningham and Woolley each received ten years, Teeters two years and Loo just one year. 'It didn't sound good,' commented Cunningham, 'but it was a lot better than being shot. We almost beamed at the senior officer.'[17] In fact, these sentences appear to be remarkably lenient when compared with other cases of recaptured Allied POWs, and the initially amused attitude of the *Kempeitai* shortly after their apprehension in Pootung may explain the non-fatal sentences. Seven days later the prisoners were removed to Ward Road Goal, an old British prison in Shanghai, where they were to serve out their sentences.

At Ward Road the escapers were in for an initially uncomfortable time, since the Japanese now commanded the facility, having interned the former British warders alongside the Caucasian officers of the Shanghai Municipal Police (SMP). The new prison governor was a Japanese named Tsugai, a former SMP officer. The prisoners were forced to relinquish their military uniforms in exchange for prison garb. They spent between eighteen and twenty hours a day locked up in their cells, though the conditions were a slight improvement over those at Kiangwan and Bridge House. The escapees could write one letter home each month and receive short notes from their families, but as punishment for having escaped from Woosung they were denied tobacco or any packages.

On 9 July 1942 four US Marines joined Smith, Cunningham and the others. Corporals Connie Battles, Charles Brimmer and Jerold Story, along with Private First Class Charles Stewart, had escaped from Woosung Camp on 31 March 1942. Like Smith and the naval escapees, the US Marines had been picked up just over two weeks later on 17 April, having failed to find any assistance from the local population. Like the first escapees, the marines were placed on trial for 'desertion'. 'We had no counsel during our trial for escaping from Woosung,' wrote Corporal Story. 'When the trial was over we were informed that Battles, Stewart and I were sentenced to four years in prison and that Brimmer was sentenced to seven years. Brimmer had admitted that he was the ring-leader of the escape. Actually this was not the case, but Brimmer admitted to the fact to stop the beatings.' Unlike Commander Smith's group, the *Kempeitai* had subjected the US Marines to extensive physical abuse at Bridge House. We can only surmise that the attitude of the Japanese to escape attempts had hardened since the recapture of Smith and his party, and when it became known amongst the other POWs that the Japanese severely beat prisoners who tried to escape, it would have had an undoubted effect on future escape attempts. 'When they told Brimmer that he got seven years, we all started to laugh and told him he would be an old man before he left the prison,' recalled Story. 'As we started to walk out of the courthouse the Japs called us back and raised Brimmer's sentence to nine years, evidently because we had laughed.'[18] In July 1943, another Caucasian prisoner was added to the escapees who were mouldering away at Ward Road Jail. Patrick Herndon, an American civilian, was sentenced to two years imprisonment for fighting with other prisoners at Woosung.

During his imprisonment Commander Cunningham's thoughts turned once more to escape. No one had ever managed to break out of Ward Road Goal, but the plucky American decided that he must try. But a bad bout of diarrhoea put paid to his plans for the time being. By February 1944 Cunningham's physical condition had deteriorated badly, with his weight down from 185 to just 129 pounds. A doctor diagnosed nervous indigestion and Cunningham was sent to the Shanghai Police Hospital for three weeks treatment during February and March. On his return to Ward Road, a new rule meant that prisoners were allowed to buy food through the Swiss Consulate, so his health improved markedly, and by September his weight was up to 167 pounds.

In May 1944 another two American servicemen arrived at Ward Road, having each been sentenced to two years imprisonment following an attempted escape from Woosung Camp. US Marine Sergeant Coulson and US Navy Pharmacist's Mate Second Class

Brewer soon after joined the growing intrigue that circulated around Commanders Smith and Cunningham concerning the planning of a fresh escape attempt.

Two Danish prisoners named Petersen and Olafsen were released from Ward Road in September 1944. Cunningham had arranged for them to sling a bag containing hacksaws over the perimeter wall at an agreed time and place. But Cunningham's plans were thrown into some disarray by an internal squabble among the would-be escapers. Smith had formed his own faction that consisted of himself, Woolley and Story. It appears that Smith had made a separate deal with the Dane Petersen, and Smith was the first to receive some hacksaws. Although Cunningham's group was able to obtain tools as well from Petersen, Smith's group was given a head start and began making preparations to escape immediately. It was only Cunningham's strident opposition that eventually convinced Smith to work together with his superior officer, especially after Cunningham pointed out during a heated exchange that Naval Headquarters would not have looked favourably upon Smith if he had left the commander of Wake Island languishing in a Japanese prison.

Eventually, and after much wrangling and argument, Smith and Woolley asked Cunningham to join their group, but Cunningham argued that all eight Americans should join, something Smith was not keen on. After more negotiations the agreed solution was for Smith's group to break out of the prison first. Cunningham's group (consisting of Cunningham, Brewer, Brimmer and Stewart) would follow behind one hour later. Corporal Battles elected to remain behind because of illness.

Initially, the plan worked perfectly. Smith's group removed their cell window bars, weakened by days of covert sawing with the illicit hacksaws, and went over the perimeter wall undetected. They headed off across country and successfully made contact with Nationalist Chinese guerrillas. Smith, Woolley and Story would travel on foot and by sampan for an astounding 700 miles into the Chinese interior, dodging Japanese patrols and betrayal at every turn, until they were passed on to Nationalist territory and freedom.

Cunningham's group was less fortunate. They also managed to escape from the prison, but after making it on foot to Suzhou

Creek, the tributary of the Huangpu River that flows through Shanghai, they were cornered and captured by Chinese police. It must have been a crushing psychological blow for Cunningham, to have successfully escaped from Japanese prisons twice and failed to get away.

The consequences of this escape were to be somewhat different from those of his previous attempt with Commander Smith in 1942. The *Kempeitai* removed Cunningham's group to Bridge House, and the two Danes, Petersen and Olafsen, were arrested and tortured.

Cunningham was thrown into a small cell that overflowed with Chinese prisoners, fed a very limited diet and had to endure filth and body lice as washing was strictly forbidden. On 3 November 1944 Cunningham was transferred to Kiangwan Military Prison where he endured eleven weeks of solitary confinement, causing his intestinal disorder to reassert itself. His weight dropped to 115 pounds and he started to develop the tropical deficiency disease beriberi. 'The only thing that gave me cheer during the frightful winter of 1944–45 were the bombings of the prison area. Eight days after I arrived at the prison the bombs started falling. Some were close enough to shake the building.'[19] Shanghai was targetted several times by American B-25 bombers during the latter part of the war.

On 11 December 1944 Cunningham's group, plus the Danes Petersen and Olafsen, were hauled before another court martial. Cunningham received a life sentence for his latest escape attempt. 'I was relieved that it wasn't death,' he wrote. 'This was the third time that I faced hard looking Japanese Army officers.'[20] Corporal Brimmer also received a life sentence – it later emerged that the *Kempeitai* had tortured him into making an admission that he was the group's ringleader. Stewart, Brewer and Coulson each received eight years imprisonment, while Petersen and Olafsen were found guilty of having aided and abetted the escape and they were sent back to Ward Road Jail for two years each.

Cunningham and his group did not remain in Shanghai for long. On 19 January 1945, in the depths of a freezing winter, Cunningham and his companions were placed aboard a train that chugged its way several hundred miles inland to the old Nationalist capital at Nanking. 'I weighed about 115 pounds and suffered increasingly from my stomach,' remembered Cunningham. 'I was starting to lose the will to live.'[21] After a further period of solitary confinement in Nanking Military Prison, Cunningham was placed in a cell with Pat Herndon, his old comrade from Ward Road Jail who had been imprisoned for fighting, and Corporal Battles. But although extremely sick and underweight the Japanese did not spare him from punishment.

On 25 June 1945, less than a month before the end of the war, the Japanese found Cunningham guilty of having been present in a cell when a window was broken. Although not guilty of having damaged the windowpane, Cunningham was fitted around the waist with a thick leather belt to which his two hands were securely lashed for *fifteen* days.

In the spring of 1945 the precarious health of Captain Cunningham (for he had been promoted *in absentia* by the US Navy, backdated to 1943) began to improve. The visible signs of the impending end of the war also lifted his spirits, not the least of which were the American bombing raids on Nanking. The Japanese sent their white prisoners, including four of Colonel Doolittle's famous flyers, to Beijing (which at this time was called Beiping) by train on 1 August 1945. Cunningham sat handcuffed to another prisoner throughout the forty-six hour journey.

On arrival in Beijing, Cunningham was sent once again to solitary confinement in a military prison until 18 August 1945. On 13 August, Cunningham noticed that the Japanese were burning huge piles of documents. 'We deduced that the Japanese were burning records, and our spirits soared,'[22] wrote Cunningham. Although the Japanese surrendered on 15 August, it was three days later before Cunningham and the other prisoners were brought before the camp commandant and informed of this momentous news. Standing stiffly before them, the rather crestfallen Japanese officer launched into a short speech. 'The war is over,' stated the commandant, adding rather optimistically, 'We hope the Americans and the Japanese will shake hands and become friends again.'[23] Cunningham and his friends were immediately moved to a civilian internment camp located at Fengtian, west of Beijing. 'Before I turned in for the night, I took a stroll around the camp. It was something I had not been able to do for three years and eight months,' recalled Cunningham. 'I reveled in the sight of the stars, not just a few as seen through a barred window, but all of them. For the first time I could walk as long as I liked and stay up as late as I chose. Glorying in this apparently trifling privilege, I found myself realising at last that I was free.'[24]

An Army Emergency Liaison Team made contact with the inmates at Fengtian on 23 August. The next day Captain Cunningham boarded a B-24 Liberator and flew to Xian in western China. On the 25th he flew on to the Nationalist capital at Chongqing, before embarking on a journey home that would take him halfway around the world via Kunming, Calcutta, Agra, Karachi, Abidjan, Cairo, Tripoli, Casablanca, the Azores and Newfoundland, eventually arriving in New York City on 7 September 1945. The next day Cunningham arrived home at his house in Annapolis, Maryland, to the embraces of his wife and children.

In 1946 Cunningham received a Presidential Unit Citation and the Bronze Star for his defence of Wake. He would return to China one last time in 1947 when he commanded the USS *Curtiss* and put into the east coast port of Qingdao. Winfield Cunningham retired from the US Navy in 1950 with the rank of rear admiral and died in Memphis, Tennessee in March 1986 at the age of eighty-six.

Chapter 8

March into Oblivion

To think that a man was going to survive. You saw these men every day when you were getting treated for ulcers. The dead lying there, naked skeletons. They were all ready to be buried. You thought to yourself, well, how could I possibly get out of a place like this? We're in the middle of Borneo, we're in the jungle. How possibly could we ever survive?

Private Nelson Short, Australian Army

The Sandakan Death March has come to symbolise the true horror of Allied captivity in the hands of the Japanese. The terrible story of Japan's POWs is bookended by two death marches, Bataan in 1942 and Sandakan in 1945. In between lies three and a half years of starvation, torture, murder and massacre. Bataan was a movement of prisoners into camps that involved horrendous brutality on the part of the guards involved. Sandakan was a series of marches into oblivion for thousands of British and Australian soldiers who were already nearing the end of their tether after years of brutal imprisonment. It was a march to nowhere except a cold grave in the dark brown earth of the island of Borneo. We only know about this horrific crime today because somehow a tiny handful of prisoners managed to survive and later gave evidence against their Japanese tormentors. They only survived because they escaped – and such was their desperate plight that they all expected, even chose, to die as free men in the jungle rather than be murdered by the Japanese. But survive they did, against a mountain of odds that were stacked against them. The figures are truly astounding: 2,776 British and Australian POWs were imprisoned at the Sandakan camps and only *six* made it home. This is their incredible story.

In Chapter 4 the story of how the Japanese shipped in thousands of British and Australian POWs from Singapore to Borneo to work as slave labour was told. One of the POWs' primary jobs was constructing and maintaining Sandakan Airstrip. We saw that amongst the prisoners there developed a resistance group led by the indefatigable and lion-hearted Captain Lionel Matthews of the Australian Army Signal Corps. This fledgling resistance and escape organisation was betrayed to the Japanese and largely destroyed, and Matthews and his co-conspirators executed.

The fate of the prisoners in the three Sandakan camps was completely tied to the continuing useful operation of the airstrip. During the first year of their captivity at Sandakan only six POWs had died, indicating that conditions inside the camps were at least bearable, and that the Japanese authorities were carefully preserving their labour force after all the time and trouble spent getting them to Borneo from Singapore. By the time the Allies had begun to fight back across the Pacific, rations at the Sandakan camps had been severely reduced as the Japanese found it increasingly difficult to feed the prisoners. In fact, the Japanese Army was hoarding food for itself as it prepared to fend off an Allied invasion of Borneo that was expected at any time. Although the Allies had no firm plans to invade Borneo, preferring to bypass and isolate the island, suppressing Japanese air power was a vital task to prevent any interference with other operations, and these aerial operations directly contributed to the horrors that were to come.

Sandakan Airstrip came under constant attack, to the point where Japanese aircraft could no longer safely use it. With the abandonment of the airstrip the requirement to keep thousands of Allied POWs as slave labourers effectively evaporated. They were now surplus to requirements, and in the brutal logic of the Japanese military that meant only one possible fate.

In mid-1944 the Japanese examined the possibility of moving military supplies inland and across to the west coast of Borneo when it became obvious that their supply ships were being sunk. American and Australian submarines were taking a heavy toll of Japanese merchant vessels, and Allied aircraft had virtual air superiority over the island. Any Japanese plane flying supplies into the Borneo garrison was liable to fall victim to USAAF P-38 Lightnings or Royal Australian Air Force Bristol Beaufighters. The Japanese realised that they faced enormous logistical problems in trying to move hundreds of tons of food, ammunition and equipment across the rugged and hostile northeast Borneo. The British and Australian POWs would have one last task to complete before they were disposed of.

The Japanese turned for help to the pre-war British District Officer at Telupid, Mr Moore-Willie, as well as a local village headman, and told them to cut a trail from Sandakan to the small town of Ranau. The Japanese were completely dependent upon Moore-Willie and the village headman and gave them an armed Japanese escort to complete this task. For his part, Moore-Willie assumed that only the Japanese would use the route he had been instructed to make. With this in mind, he set about creating the most difficult route possible between Sandakan and Ranau through mangrove swamp, dense jungle and over mountains, fording the widest parts of major rivers, the overall idea being to slow down the movement of Japanese forces and supplies into the interior of the island.

It was one of the cruel ironies of an exceptionally cruel campaign. Moore-Willie and his native helpers had absolutely no idea that the Japanese would use almost 3,000 Allied prisoners to move their supplies and equipment – one can only imagine his horror and sorrow on discovering that he had been duped by the Japanese and he was now, though no fault of his own, indirectly contributing to the deaths of his own countrymen.

In accordance with the sudden reduction in work as the Allied air campaign closed the airstrip, in December 1944 the Japanese camp commandant, Captain Susumi Hoshijima, reduced the prisoners' already meagre rations to only 140–200 grams of food per man per day. The POW death rate, which was already fairly high from tropical diseases and physical abuse, began to climb rapidly as the men, wracked by malaria, dysentery and beriberi, now became seriously malnourished and started to die of starvation and disease in large numbers. To make matters even worse Hoshijima ordered his men to cease feeding the prisoners altogether from January 1945. The remaining British and Australian officers had overseen the hoarding of as much rice as possible for just such an eventuality, but the supply was necessarily limited and the prisoners now had to make do with only 85 grams of food per man per day. Without intervention of some kind every one of the POWs would soon die.

The Japanese high command, believing the Allied aerial campaign against Sandakan was a prelude to an invasion, decided to prevent the liberation of the remaining prisoners. This decision reflected the official Japanese policy of moving the prisoners inland to Ranau along the Moore-Willie trail whilst simultaneously using them as pack animals. The Japanese knew huge numbers of the prisoners, in a starved and diseased state, would perish along the way, but this was viewed as an added bonus, alleviating them of having to murder *en masse* the prisoners once the march was over.

What local Japanese commanders set in motion was one of the greatest crimes committed by Japan against prisoners during the Second World War. The camps were evacuated and the prisoners force-marched 260km along the Moore-Willie trail to Ranau. Any prisoners who fell out of the march were shot or bayoneted to death by special killing squads of Japanese soldiers who were ordered to deal with stragglers with the utmost severity.

There was a central contradiction in Japanese policy concerning what to do with Allied POWs in the event of an invasion. Preserving POWs as labour was seen as a short-term benefit, and this was highlighted in a Japanese government document dated 11 March 1945, which states: '... the location of camps will be changed as much as possible, and we shall not let prisoners of war fall into enemy hands until we have got some results from them.' The document also states that when moving prisoners 'emergency measures shall be taken without delay against those of antagonistic attitudes, and we shall hope for nothing regrettable by taking proper measures to suit the occasion.'[1] What this paragraph actually did was to give army commanders on the ground permission to kill the prisoners in their charge, but substituting the word 'murder' with what had been euphemistically, and vaguely, termed 'proper measures' by Tokyo. They were to make sure that no physical evidence of these crimes be left for Allied investigators to discover. If a commandant believed his prisoners were going to be liberated, he should kill them.

The terrain that the diseased and emaciated prisoners were ordered to traverse would have taxed even the fittest of soldiers, as was Moore-Willie's original and carefully devised intention. For the first three miles after leaving Sandakan the prisoners had to wade through a mangrove swamp that was teeming with mosquitoes, blood-sucking leeches and poisonous snakes. Then there followed forty miles of high ground, which consisted in the main of short, steep hills covered with secondary jungle and bisected by several sizeable rivers. After this had been negotiated the prisoners faced forty-two miles of serious mountain country before eventually descending to Ranau. The average daily march was supposed to be six and a half miles, but most of the POWs could barely manage a mile before collapsing exhausted and semi-conscious.

Each group of prisoners was divided into fifty-man parties that were issued a 100-pound bag of rice by the Japanese. This food was supposed to be sufficient to keep enough of them alive to haul Japanese kit. A leader, usually an officer or senior NCO prisoner, was issued with a sheet of paper and a pencil and told to make a roll of the prisoners in his charge. As well as their own meagre kit and food supplies, the POWs lugged Japanese military equipment and food. Accompanying each fifty-man party was one Japanese officer, three NCOs and fifteen privates, each armed with Arisaka rifles with fixed bayonets.

The first party to be marched out of Sandakan consisted of 455 Australians split into nine separate groups that left between 29 January and 6 February 1945. The Japanese cynically told them that food awaited them at the new camp at Ranau. Each man was to carry four days rations, and they were also heavily loaded with rice sacks, ammunition boxes and other Japanese military equipment. Most were barefoot, their ammunition boots having long ago disintegrated. As they began following the trail, Japanese guards in rain capes trudged along beside them. The weather was appalling, heavy rain turning large sections of the track into a muddy and slippery quagmire.

Groups 1–5 began the trek with 265 men between them, but seventy died on the journey, mostly shot or bayoneted by their guards after they collapsed. 'When we were about a week away from Ranau we crossed a large mountain,' recalled Private Keith Botterill of the 2/19th Australian Infantry Battalion who was part of this first death march, 'and while we were making the crossing two Australians, Private Humphries and a corporal whose name I cannot remember, fell out. They were suffering from beri-beri, malaria and dysentery and just could not continue any further. A Japanese private shot the corporal, and a Japanese sergeant shot Humphries. Altogether we lost five men on that hill.'[2] Botterill, a Katoomba textile printer who had enlisted in August 1941, somehow found the energy to keep going, 'I've seen men shot and bayoneted to death because they could not keep up with the party ... But I just kept plodding along. It was dense jungle, I was heartbroken; but I thought there was safety in numbers. I just kept going.'[3]

'As we were going along men would fall out as they became too weak to carry on,' recalled Botterill. 'We would march on and then, shortly afterwards, hear shots ring out and the sound of men screaming.'[4] The suffering witnessed by young soldiers like Botterill was unbelievable. 'No effort whatsoever was made to bury the men. The Japanese would just pull them five to fifteen yards off the track and bayonet or shoot them, depending on the condition of the men,' recalled Botterill. 'If they were conscious, and it was what we thought was a good, kind guard, they'd shoot them. There was nothing we could do.'[5]

Group 3, like all the other groups only carrying rations for four days, took *seventeen* days to reach Ranau and of the original fifty men who constituted this group, only thirty-seven made it. The rest were shot or bayoneted and their bodies hastily interred just off the trail by press-ganged locals.

Groups 6–9 marched to Paginatan near Ranau, and out of 200 only 138 reached their destination. Lance Bombardier William Moxham of the 2/15th Australian Field Regiment was with Group 7:

Men from my party could not go on. Boto was the first place where we actually had to leave anyone. They remained there, at this Jap dump. At the next place, at the bottom of a big hill, we left two more men. Later, we heard shots, and we thought the two men must have been shot ... Once you stopped – you stopped for good.[6]

They were held at Paginatan for one month until ordered to resume the march to Ranau. 'One man was puffed up with beriberi in the legs and face,' recalled Moxham, a 28-year-old former station overseer from Toongabbie, New South Wales, 'and he was getting along all right on his own and could have made it; but the Japs would not let him alone, but tried to force him along, and eventually he collapsed.' The Japanese guards kicked the man on the ground. 'The Jap turned and saw the man had gone down, and he struck him over the head with his rifle butt. The soldier was left there. The party marched on.'[7] Sixty-eight were still alive at this stage, and by the time they struggled into Ranau this number had been reduced to forty-six.

On arrival at Ranau there was little respite for the prisoners. They were herded into unsanitary and crowded huts. There was dirt and flies everywhere and soon a dysentery epidemic struck the already diseased and starved prisoners. 'You'd wake up of a morning and you'd look to your right to see if the chap next to you was still alive,' recalled Keith Botterill. 'If he was dead you'd just roll him over a little bit and see if he had any belongings that would suit you; if not, you'd just leave him there. You'd turn on the other side and check your neighbour; see if he was dead or alive.'[8]

Many of the prisoners at Ranau naturally harboured thoughts of escape from their hellish existence. But for most of them such dreams remained just that – they were not in the condition to disappear into the jungle, and they were far behind enemy lines. The POWs were dealt a sharp reminder of how dangerous escape could be after they witnessed what the fates were of two young Australians who had managed to slip out of the camp in March 1945. The treatment that was meted out to the two men plumbed the depths of human depravity and revealed the disgusting lengths to which the Japanese could go to punish those who broke their regulations.

Gunners Albert Cleary and Wally Crease of the 2/15th Australian Field Regiment had managed to remain on the run for four agonising days before they were recaptured. Gunner Cleary was the first to be brought back to Ranau Camp, and his face already showed the marks of the vicious beating that had been meted out to him by the Japanese immediately after his apprehension. Cleary was taken to one of the POW barrack blocks known as the 'Guard House'. One part of the block was sectioned off and served as an interrogation suite.

Cleary's arms were tied up high behind his back and he was made to kneel with a log tied behind his knees. Japanese soldiers then punched and kicked Cleary all over his body. Sometimes one guard held his head while another punched Cleary in the throat. At other times guards with rifles and fixed bayonets would charge screaming at Cleary, stopping only when their razor-sharp bayonets were inches from his face. This went on for three and a half hours, witnessed by many of the prisoners. Cleary was made to stand up every half an hour so that blood would rush into his numb lower limbs causing him extreme pain, much to the amusement of the guards. The beatings continued unabated, with rifle butts, bamboo sticks and anything else the guards could lay their hands on.

Incredibly, Gunner Cleary managed to stay alive through all of this abuse and torture. One prisoner who witnessed Cleary's sufferings and who later escaped from Ranau was Australian Private Keith Botterill. The next morning Botterill watched the Japanese start to beat Cleary again, and when Botterill returned from a working party at noon the Japanese were still abusing him.

Gunner Crease appeared back at Ranau under armed escort and together with Cleary he was brutally tortured during the rest of the day and all through the night. The sounds of violence and of Crease and Cleary's pleading with the guards to stop would stay with Keith Botterill for the rest of his life. The next morning, somehow, Wally Crease managed to escape again, hobbling painfully off into the jungle in a hopeless attempt at freedom. It may also have been a case of suicide, and if so it was successful. The circumstances of his second escape are not known, but Botterill recorded that the Japanese soon caught up with him and shot him. Considering what was to happen to Cleary, the execution of Crease was a mercy.

Private Botterill was sent away from Ranau for four days on a work detail, but when he returned he discovered that Gunner Cleary was now tied to a tree by his neck. He was still just about clinging to life but covered in bruises, cuts and dried blood. He was suffering from dysentery, but the Japanese just left him to sit in his own mess, dressed only in a filthy *fundoshi*, a Japanese cloth undergarment that most of the POWs also wore in the heat. Every so often a passing Japanese guard would bash the semi-conscious Cleary with his fist or the butt of his rifle for no reason other than sadistic pleasure.

Botterill estimated that Cleary endured between eleven and twelve days of this treatment before the Japanese realised that he was dying and they cut him down. A group of guards tossed Cleary into the gutter that ran beside the main camp road as though he was simply a bag of rubbish. To the assembled POW witnesses they stated several times: 'If you escape the same thing will happen to you.'

The Japanese, having lost interest in Cleary, eventually permitted him to be taken away by his fellow prisoners. A group of Australians carefully carried him down to a stream and washed away the filth and blood before carrying him to a bed in one of the huts where he could die peacefully among his friends. On 20 March 1945 Albert Cleary passed away at the age of 22. Today at Ranau a memorial to Cleary and Crease has been erected.

By the beginning of April 1945 only 241 prisoners were still alive at Ranau out of the 455 who had originally left the Sandakan camps. At the end of the month another eighty-nine had died at the Ranau camp, and another twenty-one perished hauling bags of rice to Paginatan to feed future evacuation parties leaving Sandakan. These 131 survivors at Ranau were reduced to only *six* by 26 June 1945.

At Sandakan Camp, starvation, disease and physical abuse had killed 885 British and Australian prisoners. In April 1945 the Japanese decided to move the remaining 'fit' POWs to Ranau, commencing a second death march. This march began in May when 800 POWs were 'evacuated' from the three camps and the Japanese burned all of the buildings down. Five hundred and thirty of these POWs were sent on the march to Ranau while the rest languished in the remains of the camps with little to eat, no shelter from the sun and rain and no hope of relief.

The second group of marchers was similarly sub-divided into several smaller parties as the first had been. They were in an even worse state than the first party that had departed several months before. For example, Group 2, which consisted of fifty men, lost twelve dead on the very first day of the march.

Among the second group to make the trek from Sandakan to Ranau were five Australians who were determined to survive. These Australians had carefully watched the behaviour of their Japanese guards, looking for a window of opportunity when they could duck off the trail and disappear in the jungle. Their plan was simple – head for the coast and hope for some sort of rescue. All five men were severely malnourished and riddled with tropical diseases. Their escape was nothing short of a miracle. But reaching ultimate salvation was to prove a challenge so great that most of them did not make it.

On 7 June 1945 Allied aircraft appeared over the marching column, as they had done on several occasions before, and the Japanese guards, fearing a strafing or bombing attack, immediately ran off into the jungle to hide, abandoning their prisoners for a few precious minutes. Gunner Owen Campbell, a 29-year-old former labourer from Brisbane who had enlisted in the Royal Australian Artillery in 1940 and had been captured along with the entire 2/10th Field Regiment in Singapore in February 1942, fled into a different part of the jungle along with four equally ill and thin companions. They slid down a 61-metre bank and hid themselves in bracken and rubbish, and lay quiet until the column had re-formed and marched on.

Each man was dressed in the remnants of his tropical uniform, many with tatty bush hats and disintegrating ammunition boots or bare feet. 'We took along 12 tins of rice, six tins of salmon and some dried fish – all stolen from the Japanese,'[9] recalled Campbell. Escaping with Campbell was Corporal Ted Emmet and Privates Keith Costin and Edward 'Ted' Skinner of the 2/10th Field Ambulance, Australian Army Medical Corps, and Private Sidney

Webber, Royal Australian Army Service Corps. They hobbled painfully after Campbell, carrying their small supply of tinned food in their haversacks. 'We also had some fish lines and a compass which Emmet had kept since our capture at Singapore in 1942,'[10] wrote Campbell.

The main problem for Campbell's group was their ill health. Years of brutal imprisonment and starvation at Sandakan had reduced them to walking skeletons. Malaria, dysentery and beri-beri added to their misery. The 8 June 1945 was their first full day of freedom since 14 February 1942, but the group only managed to painfully hobble a couple of miles through the jungle towards the coast before exhaustion and sickness stopped them in their tracks. The following day Campbell had an attack of malaria severe enough that he could not walk any further and the whole group rested up. On 10 June Campbell felt sufficiently recovered to try again, but this time Ted Skinner's dysentery meant that another member of their party was immobilised and once again the group rested in the jungle. The next morning 'I was pretty sick with beri beri and stayed with Ted,' recalled Campbell. 'Emmet, Webber and Costin pressed on to the coast.'[11]

It does not appear that the Japanese were actively hunting for the missing Australian POWs. They were probably not even missed off the line of march because so many died or were murdered along the way that it was difficult for the Japanese to keep count.

It took the second Sandakan death marchers twenty-six days to arrive at Ranau. Out of the 530 POWs who had begun the trek, only 183 made it there alive (142 Australians and 41 British). The men who died had often faced their end bravely, as recalled 27-year-old Sydneysider Private Nelson Short of 2/18th Australian Battalion:

And if blokes just couldn't go on, we shook hands with them, and said, you know, hope everything's all right. But they knew what was going to happen. There was nothing you could do. You just had to keep yourself going. More or less survival of the fittest.[12]

Brisbane-born Bombardier Richard 'Dick' Braithwaite, a 27-year-old NCO from the 2/15th Australian Field Regiment, had been so ill with malaria at the start of the march that his comrades had had to hold him up for roll call each morning. Once he had recovered from his latest bout of malaria Braithwaite decided, much as Campbell had also done, that to remain with the column meant certain death. He therefore decided to escape, but unlike Campbell he would do so alone.

At one point during the march Braithwaite took advantage of a gap in the strung-out column and he quickly slipped behind a fallen tree until everyone had passed by. Once night fell he made his way to a river that he had previously crossed with the column, hoping to follow it to the coast. Braithwaite instead encountered a sick Japanese guard who had been left behind by the column to rest and Braithwaite, though ill and half-starved, managed to kill the Japanese with his bare hands. (The Japanese recorded that they themselves lost 100 soldiers during the Sandakan Death Marches, nearly all from disease.)

Moving on through the gloom Braithwaite ended up in the middle of a jungle swamp. He appeared trapped. 'I had nowhere to go because of the gloom, and the surrounding vegetation was all heavy jungle, thorny,' he recalled. 'I just sat down on a log there and watched those reptiles, insects, crawling past, thinking, well, this is where it happens, mate, you're finished.'[13] But the will to live was strong inside Braithwaite. 'About half an hour just sitting, all of a sudden I thought, no, you're not finished. You're not going to die in a place like this. And I became really angry. I just put my head down like a bull and charged that jungle, and, I don't know, it just seemed to part. Maybe someone was looking after me.'[14]

Braithwaite summoned up every last ounce of energy that he had, and managed to reach the Lubok River and salvation. An elderly native named Abing took Braithwaite in his canoe to his village where the villagers cared for the exhausted Australian and bravely hid him from the Japanese. It was a massive risk for the locals, for if the Japanese had discovered Braithwaite in the village they would have killed everyone as punishment. According to Braithwaite, Abing and his neighbours helped him primarily because they wanted Braithwaite to tell the Allies to stop strafing their villages and canoes in their hunt for Japanese targets. To this end, they determined to reunite Braithwaite with Allied forces.

Native guides paddled Braithwaite, who was hidden under banana leaves, for twenty hours down the Lubok River to Liberon Island on the coast. On 15 June, Braithwaite's 28th birthday, he was rescued by a US Navy PT boat and taken to hospital on Tawi Tawi Island. A week later an Australian colonel visited him when he was still lying on his sick bed and told him that they were going to rescue his friends. 'I can remember this so vividly,' said Braithwaite. 'I just rolled on my side in the bunk, faced the wall, and cried like a baby. And said "You'll be too late".'[15]

Gunner Campbell's party in the jungle had to be very careful because there were plenty of Japanese about, and they were not taking any prisoners. Campbell stayed with the sick Ted Skinner for three days. On the morning of 16 June Campbell found himself alone. 'I went to get some water and fish. When I came back I found Ted with his throat cut. I buried him there.' Skinner had committed suicide rather than prevent Campbell from making good his escape, Campbell recalling that his friend was a 'brave and gentle man' who always carried his Bible with him. Two days later Campbell managed to catch up with the others. 'I came to a river and found Costin, crook with dysentery and malaria, sheltering under a blanket,' wrote Campbell. 'Webber and Emmet were fishing nearby.'[16] Their situation was bleak. All of them were sick and they were running out of food. Without help they would all die in the jungle in a matter of days.

The escapees decided that they must find some help, and they decided to approach the locals. A short time later they heard some natives coming down the river in a sampan and Emmet and Webber went off to hail them. 'As the boat approached a Jap stood up from the bottom of the boat and fired four shots killing both Emmet and Webber. It was so quick they had no chance and fell in the river.' Fortunately, Campbell was some way behind Emmet and Webber when the shooting began and the Japanese soldier never saw him, 'so I escaped and went back to Jack Costin.'[17]

With their escape party now reduced to just two ill and starving men, Campbell and Costin stayed put for a further three days.

'We lived on fish, which I caught from the river, and fungus which grows on the trees there.' Campbell realised that Costin was slipping away. 'Jack was getting very weak at this stage and he died on the evening of 21 June. I buried him as best I could.'[18] Alone, Campbell was determined not to die in the dense jungle but to survive and avenge all of his comrades who had been killed in this tropical hellhole at the end of the earth. He would wander the jungle for eleven days, slipping further into a fevered and confused state.

On the first day after Costin's death, 22 June, Campbell swam across a wide river on a log. 'A Jap saw me and fired at me, hitting me on the wrist. I managed to make the shore as the Jap continued to fire at me.'[19] Campbell ran off into the jungle as Arisaka rifle rounds whizzed and cracked through the trees around him.

Three days later and Campbell was delirious with fever. 'I began to think my mates were back with me,' he recalled. 'I talked to them.'[20] On 3 July Campbell approached a river where he saw a small native canoe. 'Probably close to death, he had little choice but to take a chance of calling out to the men in the canoe,'[21] wrote war crimes investigator Major W.S. Jackson in 1947. The two natives, Gulunting and Lap, were out tending their fishing traps when they spotted a thin, dirty and bearded white man calling to them from the riverbank. 'I looked at the man and saw that he was practically naked,'[22] recalled Gulunting. 'We approached him and he commenced to faint. I got hold of him and carried him into the boat. We then went upriver to our camp and took him there.'

Campbell swam in and out of consciousness. 'I carried him to my hut where he was provided with trousers and shirt and food,' said Gulunting. For ten days the locals, at great risk, hid Campbell and tried their best to restore his health to the point where they could hand him over to local guerrillas. When Campbell was finally well enough to travel again he gave Gulunting Emmet's army compass to thank him for his kindnesses and bravery.

Campbell left Kampong Muanad in the company of two native resistance agents called Salium and Ambian. They were part of a network of guerrillas who were being armed and trained by the Services Reconnaissance Department (SRD), the Australian version of Britain's Special Operations Executive. Small SRD commando teams known as 'Force Z' were already inside northern Borneo preparing the way for an Allied invasion. They were Campbell's main chance for survival.

Meanwhile, in the smoldering ruins of the Sandakan camps the Japanese still had 288 Australian and British prisoners of war in July 1945. They were deprived of shelter from the sun and the incessant freezing rainstorms. Mid-month, the Japanese officer commanding the camp received orders to move the remaining prisoners to Ranau, again by forced march. Most were so ill and emaciated by this stage that they would have to be left behind.

The fittest seventy-five were organised and forced out onto a third death march to Ranau. None of them got further than 60km before collapsing and being executed by their guards. On 13 July the Japanese rounded up twenty-three of those who had remained behind at Sandakan and took them to the nearby abandoned airfield. Captain Takuo Takakuwa had ordered Sergeant Major Hisao Murozumi to 'dispose' of them, and Murozumi and his men executed them all by firing squad. Private Yashitoro Goto recalled:

It was Takakua's [Captain Takakuwa] order so we could not disobey. It would be a disgrace to my parents so we carried out the orders. Taking the PWs to the airport near the old house on the drome, all those who could walk ... under Morojumi's [Murozumi] order we lined them up and shot them. The firing party kept firing till there were no more signs of life. Then we dragged the bodies into a near-by air-raid shelter and filled it in.[23]

At Ranau, the death rate among the remaining prisoners had reached seven per day by July 1945. They cut bamboo, collected wood and attap for the huts, and carried 20kg bags of food to Ranau from the Japanese supply dump that was located three agonising kilometres away. Some were forced to haul an average of 130 buckets full of water up a steep hill each day to supply the Japanese officers' quarters. The rations that were issued to the prisoners were deliberately designed to kill them. 'They were given a small cup of rice water a day with about an inch of rice in the bottom,' recalled Private Keith Botterill. 'Plenty of rice was available and the Japanese used to get 800 grams a day themselves, they also used to get tapioca, meat, eggs and sweet potatoes and showed no signs of malnutrition.'[24]

Botterill and three companions, Lance Bombardier William Moxham, Private Nelson Short and Private Andy Anderson, decided to escape. All three men knew that to remain at Ranau would only have ended with their deaths. 'We picked the moment when we knew that death was a sure thing,' said Botterill. 'There was no option left: die in the camp or die in the jungle.'[25] The very slim chance of seeing their loved ones back in Australia drove these extremely sick men to cling to life.

The four Australians managed to slip out of the poorly guarded camp in mid-July. Anderson died of chronic dysentery on 29 July and was buried by the others in the jungle, but the three survivors managed to find sanctuary with sympathetic locals in early August. Led by a local village headman named Baragah, this resourceful leader was determined to deliver his three charges safely into Allied hands and he agreed to take a letter to the nearest Australian unit.

While Baragah was heading out to search for an SRD patrol, Gunner Owen Campbell, with his two native guides, had reached an SRD camp that was under the command of a Lieutenant Hollingsworth. Campbell's malaria returned and he was forced to rest for three or four days before the SRD could arrange for his rescue. Hollingsworth had Campbell dosed with quinine and tried to build him up a bit with bully beef and biscuits.

Campbell's rescue demonstrated just how militarily isolated the Japanese garrison on Borneo had become. The young Australian was loaded aboard a small native boat and taken out to sea. All the arrangements had already been made by radio between the SRD camp and the USS *Pocomoke*, an 8,950-ton seaplane tender and transport ship that was patrolling close to northeast Borneo. A seaplane landed in the water and his native guides transferred Campbell to it without incident. Within an hour Campbell was between clean sheets in the American vessel's white and antiseptic smelling infirmary and his survival finally guaranteed. The American sailors had been shocked by the sight of the bearded, emaciated, diseased Campbell as he had been helped aboard from the seaplane, a young soldier who shuffled painfully along like a man three times his age, his health destroyed by deliberate cruelty and neglect – here was the reason why they must defeat Japan.

On 18 July 1945 an SRD rescue unit from Morotai had been parachuted into a village about fifteen miles from the camp at Ranau after the Australians had learned of the plight of Allied POWs from the Sandakan death marches. Once on the ground the Australian commandos patrolled out over several weeks until they located the missing POWs through their contacts in the local community. Sergeant John 'Lofty' Hodges, a 6-foot 7-inch SRD giant eventually met up with Headman Baragah, who handed him the letter that had been written by Moxham on a page torn out of a school exercise book. 'We are three Australian prisoners of war,' began Moxham's neatly written note. 'We escaped from camp early in July as Nippon was starving all men. They were dying six and seven a day. The dusan [headman] found us and has looked after us ever since, building a little hut in the jungle. We are still very weak but OK. Baragah is a Tuan Besair [chief headman] and you will find all the dusans very sincere.'[26]

'Today they wanted me to write this note and Baragah is going to contact you,' continued Moxham's letter. 'Hope it will not be too long before I see you. To my knowledge only about ten or twenty left out of 3,000 or more ... We are anxiously awaiting to hear from you. About five miles from Ranau.'[27]

Moxham's note was sent on 17 August 1945, two days after the Japanese surrender. At Sandakan the last twenty-nine prisoners had starved to death among the ruins of the camp, and far from there being 'ten or twenty left out of 3,000' as Moxham hoped, on 15 August only one Australian prisoner was still alive. On the very day that the war ended Sergeant Major Hisao had this last prisoner murdered. Wong Hiong, a Chinese worker at the camp, witnessed the grisly scene. According to Wong the Australian soldier's 'legs were covered with ulcers. He was a tall, thin, dark man with a long face and was naked apart from a loin cloth.' The prisoner was taken to a drain. Murozumi 'made the man kneel down and tied a black cloth over his eyes,' recalled Wong. 'He did not say anything or make any protest. He was so weak that his hands were not tied. Morojumi [Murozumi] cut his head off with one sword stroke.' The Japanese then pushed the decapitated corpse into the drain where the soldier's head already lay. 'The other Japs threw in some dirt, covered the remains and returned to the camp,'[28] said Wong.

At the Ranau camp around forty British and Australian POWs managed to cling to life following the Japanese surrender – but not for long. Help in the form of an SRD unit never reached them, leaving the Japanese to destroy any evidence of their atrocities.

Shortly before that, two of the prisoners had decided to survive, come what may. Towards the end of July a friendly Japanese guard had approached Warrant Officer Class 1 Hector 'Bill' Sticpewich with a warning. The Japanese told Sticpewich that all of the remaining prisoners were soon to be executed. Early the following morning, 28 July 1945, Sticpewich and Private Herman 'Algy' Reither slipped out of Ranau Camp, went a short way up a road and hid in the brush until the Japanese gave up searching for them. The two men moved on and were eventually taken in by a local Christian, Dihil bin Ambilid. Risking his life, Ambilid did not betray Sticpewich and Reither to the Japanese, even though they had offered sizeable rewards to any native who captured and handed over escaped Allied POWs. Instead, Ambilid fed the two Australians. Hearing of SRD troops in the vicinity, Ambilid took a message to them, bringing back medicines and food. Unfortunately, during the days that Ambilid was on his mercy mission, Private Reither had died of dysentery and malnutrition. An SRD team eventually rescued Warrant Officer Sticpewich shortly after the Japanese surrender.

On 27 August 1945, twelve days *after* the Japanese surrender, the last forty survivors at Ranau were each shot in the back of the head by Japanese soldiers. Three days before this outrage, Sergeant Hodges' SRD unit finally rescued Moxham, Botterill and Short. The three Australian escapees were hobbling painfully along a jungle trail at the head of a group of villagers. Botterill was a dirty and bearded bag of bones, wracked with malaria and with a scrotal sac that was so distended with beriberi that the only way he could walk was by supporting his private parts with a knapsack. Short, likewise, looked as though his limbs had been inflated, so bad was his beriberi. 'How ya going, boys?' was the first thing the three men heard as a smiling Hodges stepped out of the bush behind them. The enormous sergeant, with his jungle green combat uniform and carbine that looked almost like a toy cradled in his huge hands, was an impressive sight. Hodges offered them tea, milk, sugar, biscuits and chocolate, which none of the men had seen since leaving Changi Camp in Singapore over three years before. Both Botterill and Short wept openly. 'It was wonderful. I'll never forget it. We all sat down and had a cup of tea together,'[29] recalled Short. Moxham and Botterill were carried on stretchers to Hodges' camp. Nelson Short, even though in extreme discomfort, stubbornly walked there. 'Nelson was so bloated,' recalled Hodges, 'but I thought Keith [Botterill] was the worst. I picked him up like a little baby he was so emaciated.'[30]

For three weeks Hodges cared for Botterill as though he was his child. He carried him to the latrine, bathed him in the nearby creek, fed him and administered his medicines. 'I was only a comparative youngster, but I felt that this should happen to a fellow Australian soldier was too much,' said Hodges. 'Then my reaction was just one of anger. I must confess I wore that anger for years afterwards.' Hodges' fury found an avenue when two Japanese prisoners came into his camp and then made the mistake of trying to escape. Hodges picked one up bodily and threw him to the ground like a rag doll – the other he laid out cold with his fists. Considering the scale of the war crimes committed at Sandakan and Ranau, it is a wonder that the Australians took any Japanese prisoners at all.

Altogether 2,776 Australian and British prisoners had been brought to Sandakan in three large shipments as slave labourers. Only *six* Australians ultimately survived, making the Sandakan Death Marches amongst the worst war crimes committed by the Japanese against Allied forces during the Second World War. It was only because six men managed to survive that the world eventually learned of what the Japanese had done at Sandakan. The testimony provided by Botterill, Short, Campbell, Moxham, Sticpewich and Braithwaite to Australian war crimes investigators ensured that some degree of retribution was taken against the perpetrators. Captain Susumi Hoshijima, the homicidal Sandakan commandant, was found guilty of war crimes and executed by hanging on 6 April 1946. Captain Takakuwa was hanged alongside Hoshijima. Captain Genzo Watanabe, the second-in-command, was executed by firing squad on 16 March 1946. Fifty-five lower-ranking Japanese officers and men were found guilty of lesser counts of brutality and received terms of imprisonment. However, most of the guards who had accompanied the marches had murdered Allied POWs, and nearly all of them were never prosecuted.

For the handful of Sandakan survivors, dealing with the psychological problems caused by such a terrible ordeal must have been difficult to say the least. William Moxham, who had so resolutely walked into the SRD camp outside Ranau in August 1945, committed suicide in 1961. On the other hand Bill Sticpewich, who was awarded an MBE in 1947 for his brave activities inside the Sandakan camps, survived until 1977 when he was knocked down and killed crossing the road in Melbourne. Dick Braithwaite succumbed to cancer in 1986, Keith Botterill died of emphysema in 1997, and Nelson Short died of a heart attack in 1995. The last Sandakan survivor, Owen Campbell, died at his home in 2003 aged 87. But although all of the survivors have passed away, Sandakan has not been forgotten. It stands as a sombre reminder of Japan's wartime brutality and culture of cruelty.

'The Sandakan story has got to be brought out into the light. That's what I reckon,' wrote Owen Campbell in 1995, shortly after returning to Sandakan for the first time since his escape in 1945. 'Bring it to their [young people's] notice and then they'll start to talk and that will bring it further into the minds of the younger generation that is coming up. That's the only way I can do it. When you realise it's got to be told then you don't mind the personal anguish, as long as it does some good somewhere along the line and opens people's eyes.'[31]

Appendix A

Asia-Pacific War Timeline

1936

25 November   Japan signs the Anti-Comintern Pact with Germany

1937

7 July   Japan invades China

13 December   Start of the 'Rape of Nanking'

1939

May–August   Japanese and Soviet forces fight the Battle of Nomonhan on the Manchurian-Mongolian border and Japan is defeated

1 September   Germany invades Poland

3 September   France, Britain and the Commonwealth declare war on Germany

1940

22 June   France falls to the Germans

Japan invades and occupies French Indochina

26 June   United States places an embargo on iron and steel imports to Japan

27 September   Japan signs the Tripartite Pact with Germany and Italy

1941

10 January   Thailand invades French Indochina

22 June   Germany invades the Soviet Union

26 July	United States places an oil embargo on Japan
7 December	Japanese bomb Pearl Harbor, Wake Island, Midway Island and the Philippines
8 December	Japanese invade British Malaya, Thailand and Hong Kong
9 December	China declares war on the Axis Powers
10 December	Japan sinks the British capital ships HMS *Prince of Wales* and HMS *Repulse* off Malaya and begins landings on the Philippines
14 December	Japan invades Burma
16 December	Japan invades Borneo
20 December	Japan attacks the Netherlands East Indies
24 December	Japan occupies Wake Island after a bitter battle with US forces
25 December	Hong Kong surrenders to the Japanese

1942

3 February	Japanese forces begin landing in the Netherlands East Indies
	Japanese aircraft attack Port Moresby, New Guinea
15 February	British forces surrender to the Japanese in Singapore
	Japanese aircraft attack Darwin in Australia
27 February	Japanese Navy wins the Battle of the Java Sea
8 March	Japanese invade New Guinea
6 April	Japanese invade the Admiralty and British Solomon Islands
9 April	US forces in the Bataan Peninsula, Philippines, surrender to the Japanese
18 April	The Doolittle Raid is launched on Tokyo
1 May	Japanese forces capture Mandalay, Burma
6 May	US forces on Corregidor Island, Philippines, surrender to the Japanese
7 May	Battle of the Coral Sea
23 May	British withdrawal from Burma completed
4 June	Japanese attack Midway Island
6 June	Japanese invade the Aleutian Islands
	US Navy is victorious at The Battle of Midway

APPENDIX A

7 August	US forces land on Guadalcanal in the British Solomon Islands
9 August	Japanese Navy victorious at the Battle of Savo Island
12 August	Japanese land at Buna, New Guinea
18 September	Australian forces begin advancing down the Kokoda Trail, New Guinea
11–12 October	Japanese Navy defeated at the Battle of Cape Esperance
17 October	British forces advance into the Arakan, Burma
26 October	Japanese Navy victorious at the Battle of Santa Cruz

1943

2 February	Soviet Union wins the Battle of Stalingrad
13 February	British launch the first Chindit expedition into Burma
2 March	Battle of the Bismarck Sea
20 June	US forces invade New Georgia
3 September	Allied forces land in Italy
20 November	US forces land on Tarawa

1944

31 January	US forces land in the Marshall Islands
2 March	British launch second Chindit expedition into Burma
15 March	Japanese invade India at Imphal and Kohima
22 April	US forces land at Hollandia, New Guinea
31 May	Japanese begin withdrawing from Kohima
4 June	Allied forces capture Rome
6 June	D-Day landings in Normandy, France
15 June	US forces land on Saipan
19 June	Commencement of the Battle of the Philippine Sea
18 July	Japanese forces begin withdrawing from Imphal
15 September	US forces land on Peleliu
20 October	US forces land on Leyte, Philippines
24–25 October	Battle of Leyte Gulf
December	British 14th Army enters Burma

1945

9 January	US forces land on Luzon, Philippines
11 January	British forces cross the Irrawaddy River, Burma
19 February	US forces land on Iwo Jima
2 March	British forces capture Meiktila, Burma
20 March	British forces capture Mandalay, Burma
1 April	US forces land on Okinawa
12 April	President Roosevelt dies
30 April	Hitler dies in Berlin
3 May	British forces enter Rangoon, Burma
8 May	Germany surrenders
26 July	Churchill resigns as British Prime Minister
6 August	Atomic bomb dropped on Hiroshima, Japan – POWs beaten at Mukden
8 August	Soviet Union declares war on Japan and invades Manchuria
9 August	Atomic bomb dropped on Nagasaki, Japan
15 August	Japan announces its surrender
26 August	Soviet invasion of Manchuria complete
2 September	Formal surrender of Japan

Appendix B

Roll of Honour

British and Australian Servicemen Executed by the Japanese for Attempting to Escape[1]

1. Private Alexander Bell, 16 March 1942, Australian Army, Burma
2. Sergeant Joseph Bell, 16 September 1943, Australian Army, Malaya
3. Private Joseph Bell, 18 June 1942, Australian Army, Malaya
4. Gunner Albert Cleary, 2/15th Field Regiment, Royal Australian Artillery, Age 22, 20 March 1945, Borneo
5. Gunner Walter Crease, 2/15th Field Regiment, Royal Australian Artillery, c.8 March 1945, Borneo
6. Gunner Thomas Cumming, 4th Anti-Tank Regiment, Royal Australian Artillery, September 1942, Burma
7. Sergeant Clifford Danaher, 4th Anti-Tank Regiment, Royal Australian Artillery, September 1942, Burma
8. Private William David, 2nd (Selangor) Bn., Federated Malay States Volunteer Force, No. 13590, Age 38, 4 June 1943, Singapore
9. Warrant Officer Class 2 Leslie Davies, 22 March 1942, Australian Army, Sumatra
10. Gunner Keith Dickinson, 2 March 1943, Royal Australian Artillery, Burma
11. Lance Corporal Robin Elliott, 4th (Malacca Volunteer Corps) Bn., Straits Settlements Volunteer Corps, No. 80823, Age 28, 4 June 1943, Thailand

12. Lance Bombardier Aubrey Emmett, 4th Anti-Tank Regiment, Royal Australian Artillery, September 1942, Burma
13. Private Patrick Fitzgerald, Royal Army Ordnance Corps, No. 3651198, Age 31, 8 March 1943, Thailand
14. Private Eric Fletcher, Royal Army Ordnance Corps, No. 7591250, Age 21, 2 September 1942, Thailand
15. Gunner Alan Glover, 4th Anti-Tank Regiment, Royal Australian Artillery, September 1942, Burma
16. Signaller Howard Harvey, 11 May 1943, Australian Army Signal Corps, Borneo
17. Second Lieutenant William Harvey, Mentioned in Despatches, Federated Malay States Volunteer Force (General List), No. 68285, Age 29, 18 September 1942, Malaya
18. Gunner D. Hunter, 9th Coast Regiment, Royal Artillery, 19 March 1942, Singapore
19. Gunner G. Jeffries, 9th Coast Regiment, Royal Artillery, 19 March 1942, Singapore
20. Lance Bombardier Arthur Jones, 4th Anti-Tank Regiment, Royal Australian Artillery, September 1942, Burma
21. Sergeant Carlisle Jones, 22 March 1942, Australian Army, Sumatra
22. Sergeant Francis Kelly, Royal Army Medical Corps, No. 7259593, Age 32, 23 March 1943, Thailand
23. Fusilier Timothy Kenneally, 9th Bn., The Royal Northumberland Fusiliers, No. 4271150, Age 32, 23 March 1943, Thailand
24. Gunner J. McCann, 9th Coast Regiment, Royal Artillery, 19 March 1942, Singapore
25. Private Daniel McKenzie, 11 May 1943, Australian Army, Borneo
26. Major Alan Mull, 10 March 1943, Australian Army, Burma
27. Warrant Officer Class 2 Matthew Quittenton, 4th Anti-Tank Regiment, Royal Australian Artillery, September 1942, Burma
28. Sergeant Edward Reay, 9th Bn., The Royal Northumberland Fusiliers, No. 4269426, 23 March 1943, Thailand
29. Gunner Arthur Reeve, 4th Anti-Tank Regiment, Royal Australian Artillery, September 1942, Burma
30. Private William Schuberth, 30 July 1942, Australian Army, Malaya

31. Private James Stewart, 1st (Perak) Bn., Federated Malay States Volunteer Force, No. 13648, Age unknown, 6 June 1943, Thailand
32. Lieutenant Frank Vanrenen, Federated Malay States Volunteer Force (General List), No. 28000, Age 39, September 1942, Malaya
33. Private Harold Waters, 2nd Bn., East Surrey Regiment, No. 6140961, Age 23, 2 September 1942, Singapore
34. Gunner James Wilson, 4th Anti-Tank Regiment, Royal Australian Artillery, September 1942, Burma

Appendix C

Speech by Lieutenant Colonel Y. Nagatomo, Chief No. 3 Branch Thailand POW Administration to Allied POWs at Thanbyuzayat Camp, Burma, 28 October 1942

It is a great pleasure to me to see you at this place as I am appointed Chief of the war prisoners camp obedient to the Imperial Command issued by His Majesty the Emperor. The great East Asiatic war has broken out due to the rising of the East Asiatic Nations whose hearts were burnt with the desire to live and preserve their nations on account of the intrusion of the British and Americans for the past many years.

There is, therefore, no other reason for Japan to drive out the Anti-Asiatic powers of the arrogant and insolent British and Americans from East Asia in co-operation with our neighbors of China and other East Asiatic Nations and establish the Great East Asia Co-Prosperity Sphere for the benefit of all human beings and establish lasting great peace in the world. During the past few centuries, Nippon has made great sacrifices and extreme endeavors to become the leader of the East Asiatic Nations, who were mercilessly and pitifully treated by the outside forces of the British and Americans, and the Nippon Army, without disgracing anybody, has been doing her best until now for fostering Nippon's real power.

Appendix C

You are only a few remaining skeletons after the invasion of East Asia for the past few centuries, and are pitiful victims. It is not your fault, but until your governments do not wake up from their dreams and discontinue their resistance, all of you will not be released. However, I shall not treat you badly for the sake of humanity as you have no fighting power left at all.

His Majesty the Emperor has been deeply anxious about all prisoners of war, and has ordered us to enable the operating of War Prisoner camps at almost all the places in the southwest countries.

The Imperial Thoughts are unestimable and the Imperial Favors are infinite and, as such, you should weep with gratitude at the greatness of them. I shall correct or mend the misleading and improper Anti Japanese ideas. I shall meet with you hereafter and at the beginning I shall require of you the four following points:

(1) I heard that you complain about the insufficiency of various items. Although there may be lack of materials it is difficult to meet your requirements. Just turn your eyes to the present conditions of the world. It is entirely different from the pre-war times. In all lands and countries materials are considerably short and it is not easy to obtain even a small piece of cigarette and the present position is such that it is not possible even for needy women and children to get sufficient food. Needless to say, therefore, at such inconvenient places even our respectable Imperial Army is also not able to get mosquito nets, foodstuffs, medicines and cigarettes. As conditions are such, how can you expect me to treat you better than the Imperial Army? I do not prosecute according to my own wishes and it is not due to the expense but due to the shortage of materials at such difficult places. In spite of our wishes to meet their requirements, I cannot do so with money. I shall supply you, however, if I can do so with my best efforts and I hope you will rely upon me and render your wishes before me. We will build the railroad if we have to build it over the white man's body. It gives me great pleasure to have a fast-moving defeated nation in my power. You are merely rabble but I will not feel bad because it is [the fault of] your rulers.

If you want anything you will have to come through me for same and there will be many of you who will not see your homes again. Work cheerfully at my command.

(2) I shall strictly manage all of your going out, coming back, meeting with friends, communications. Possessions of money shall be limited, living manners, deportment, salutation, and attitude shall be strictly according to the rules of the Nippon Army, because it is only possible to manage you all, who are merely rabble, by the order of military regulations. By this time I shall issue separate pamphlets of house rules of War prisoners and you are required to act strictly in accordance with these rules and you shall not infringe on them by any means.

(3) My biggest requirement from you is escape. The rules of escape shall naturally be severe. This rule may be quite useless and only binding to some of the war prisoners, but it is most important for all of you in the management of the camp. You should, therefore, be contented accordingly. If there is a man here who has at least 1% of a chance of escape, we shall make him face the extreme penalty. If there is one foolish man who is trying to escape, he shall see big jungles toward the East which are impossible for communication. Towards the West he shall see boundless ocean and, above all, in the main points of the North, South, our Nippon Armies are guarding. You will easily understand the difficulty of complete escape. A few such cases of ill-omened matters which happened in Singapore [execution of over a thousand Chinese civilians] shall prove the above and you should not repeat such foolish things although it is a lost chance after great embarrassment.

(4) Hereafter, I shall require all of you to work as nobody is permitted to do nothing and eat at the present. In addition, the Imperial Japanese have great work to promote at the places newly occupied by them, and this is an essential and important matter. At the time of such shortness of materials your lives are preserved by the military, and all of you must award them with your labor. By the hand of the Nippon Army Railway Construction Corps to connect Thailand and Burma, the work has started to the great interest of the world. There are deep jungles where no man ever came to clear them by

cutting the trees. There are also countless difficulties and suffering, but you shall have the honor to join in this great work which was never done before, and you shall also do your best effort. I shall investigate and check carefully about your coming back, attendance so that all of you except those who are unable to work shall be taken out for labor. At the same time I shall expect all of you to work earnestly and confidently henceforth you shall be guided by this motto.

Notes

Introduction

1. Bill Young's Speech at the Burwood Sandakan Memorial Service, 5 August 2007, far-eastern-heroes.org.uk, accessed 5 June 2012
2. *Ibid.*

Chapter 1: Escape is Forbidden

1. Christopher Bayly & Tim Harper, *Forgotten Armies: Britain's Asian Empire & the War with Japan* (London: Allen Lane, 2004), 337
2. R.M. Horner, *Singapore Diary: The Hidden Journal of Captain R.M. Horner* (London: Spellmount Publishers Ltd, 2007), 14
3. *Ibid*: 310
4. 1504, Tokyo War Trials, 253;33, PX 1504, *Charles Heath, Affidavit re War Crimes at Changi Prisoner of War Camp*, 8 January 1946 (MacMillan Brown Library, University of Canterbury, New Zealand)
5. *Ibid.*
6. *Ibid.*
7. '*Brutal Story from Changi Camp*' by Athole Stewart, *The Argus*, 12 September 1945, page 3
8. 1549, Tokyo War Trials, 52;39, PX 1709, *H.D.W. Sitwell, Affidavit on Treatment in POW Camp on Java*, 10 December 1945 (MacMillan Brown Library, University of Canterbury, New Zealand)
9. *Ibid.*
10. *Ibid.*
11. *Ibid.*

12. *Ibid.*
13. *Ibid.*
14. *Ibid.*
15. Lord Russell of Liverpool, *The Knights of Bushido: A Short History of Japanese War Crimes* (London: Greenhill Books, 2002), 163
16. Oliver Lindsay, *The Battle for Hong Kong 1941–1945: Hostage to Fortune* (London: Spellmount Publishers Ltd, 2005), 174
17. Gunner Thomas Cumming, Sergeant Clifford Danaher, Lance Bombardier Aubrey Emmett, Gunner Alan Glover, Lance Bombardier Arthur Jones, Warrant Officer Class 2 Matthew Quittenton, Gunner Arthur Reeve and Gunner James Wilson
18. 'The Bridge Over the River Kwai' by Alan Brown, Children of Far East Prisoners of War, cofepow.org.uk, accessed 7 September 2012

Chapter 2: Fast Boat to China

1. *Hong Kong Escape*, hongkongescape.org/Escape, accessed 6 March 2012
2. *Ibid.*
3. *Ted Ross – Personal Papers*, hongkongescape.org/Escape, accessed 6 March 2012
4. *Ibid.*
5. *Waiapa Church Gazette*, 14 August 1943, hongkongescape.org/ Escape, accessed 12 March 2012
6. *Ted Ross – Personal Papers*, hongkongescape.org/Escape, accessed 6 March 2012
7. *David MacDougall family papers*, hongkongescape.org/Escape, accessed 6 March 2012
8. George Wright-Nooth, *Prisoner of the Turnip Heads* (London: Leo Cooper, 1994), 58
9. Richard Hide, *The 2nd MTB Flotilla's Escape from Hong Kong*, www.bbc.co.uk/history/ww2peopleswar/stories/51/a4830851.shtml, accessed 16 April 2013
10. *Ibid.*

Chapter 3: The BAAG and a Great Escape

1. Oliver Lindsay, *The Battle for Hong Kong 1941–1945: Hostage to Fortune* (London: Spellmount Publishers Ltd, 2005), 159

2. *Ibid*: 160
3. *Ibid*: 161
4. *Ibid*: 161
5. *Ibid*: 161
6. *Ibid*: 161
7. *McEwan to Elizabeth Ride*, hongkongescape.com/McEwan.htm, accessed 30 January 2012
8. M.R.D. Foot, *SOE: An Outline History of the Special Operations Executive* (London: Pimlico, 1999), 352
9. Freddie Guest, *Escape from the Bloodied Sun* (Norwich: Jarrolds, 1956), 13
10. Lord Ashcroft, *George Cross Heroes: Incredible True Stories of Bravery beyond the Battlefield* (London: Headline Review, 2010), 189
11. *Ibid*: 193
12. Oliver Lindsay, *The Battle for Hong Kong 1941–1945: Hostage to Fortune* (London: Spellmount Publishers Ltd, 2005), 173
13. *Ibid*: 173
14. Midge Gillies, *The Barbed Wire University: The Real Lives of Prisoners of War in the Second World War* (Aurum Press Ltd, 2011), 223
15. Lord Russell of Liverpool, *The Knights of Bushido: A Short History of Japanese War Crimes* (London: Greenhill Books, 2002), 122
16. Gavan Daws, *Prisoners of the Japanese: POWs of the Second World War* (London: Pocket Books, 1994), 104
17. *Ibid*: 173
18. Oliver Lindsay, *The Battle for Hong Kong 1941–1945: Hostage to Fortune* (London: Spellmount Publishers Ltd, 2005), 181
19. Ralph Goodwin, *Passport to Eternity* (London: Arthur Baker, 1956), 6
20. George Wright-Nooth, *Prisoner of the Turnip Heads* (London: Lee Cooper, 1994), 106
21. Lord Ashcroft, *George Cross Heroes: Incredible True Stories of Bravery beyond the Battlefield* (London: Headline Review, 2010), 191
22. Midge Gillies, *The Barbed Wire University: The Real Lives of Prisoners of War in the Second World War* (Aurum Press Ltd, 2011), 223

23. Lord Ashcroft, *George Cross Heroes: Incredible True Stories of Bravery beyond the Battlefield* (London: Headline Review, 2010), 192

24. Oliver Lindsay, *The Battle for Hong Kong 1941–1945: Hostage to Fortune* (London: Spellmount Publishers Ltd, 2005), 196

25. *Ibid*: 192

Chapter 4: 'This is the BBC'

1. *Tribute to east's war hero* by Adam Todd, *Eastern Courier* (Adelaide), 14 April 2010

2. *'Service Record – VX24597 – Matthews, Lionel'*, 6, National Archives of Australia. Australian Government, naa.gov.au, accessed 18 January 2012

3. *Laden, Fevered, Starved – The POWs of Sandakan, North Borneo, 1945*, Department of Veterans' Affairs, Australian Government, dva.gov.au, accessed 6 August 2008

4. *Ibid.*

5. *The Sandakan Incident*, Department of Veterans' Affairs, Australian Government, dva.gov.au, accessed 19 January 2012

6. *Ibid.*

7. *Laden, Fevered, Starved – The POWs of Sandakan, North Borneo, 1945*, Department of Veterans' Affairs, Australian Government, dva.gov.au, accessed 6 August 2008

8. *Laden, Fevered, Starved – The POWs of Sandakan, North Borneo, 1945*, Department of Veterans' Affairs, Australian Government, dva.gov.au, accessed 6 August 2008

9. *'Service Record – VX24597 – Matthews, Lionel'*, 34–36, National Archives of Australia. Australian Government, naa.gov.au, accessed 18 January 2012

10. *Ibid*: 34-36

11. *The Sandakan Incident*, Department of Veterans' Affairs, Australian Government, dva.gov.au, accessed 19 January 2012

12. *Ibid.*

13. *'Service Record – VX24597 – Matthews, Lionel'*, 34–36, National Archives of Australia. Australian Government, naa.gov.au, accessed 18 January 2012

14. Rod Wells, *Stolen Years: Australian Prisoners of War*, Australian War Memorial, awm.gov.au/stolenyears/ww2/japan/sandakan/story3.asp, accessed 17 March 2008

15. *'Service Record – VX24597 – Matthews, Lionel'*, 34–36, National Archives of Australia. Australian Government, naa.gov.au, accessed 18 January 2012
16. *Tribute to east's war hero* by Adam Todd, *Eastern Courier* (Adelaide), 14 April 2010

Chapter 5: Ten Escape from Tojo

1. *Ten Escape from Tojo* by Commander Melvin H. McCoy, USN, and Lieutenant Colonel S.M. Mellnik, USA as told to Lieutenant Welbourn Kelley, USNR, March 1944, Franklin D. Roosevelt Library and Museum, Safe Files, Box 3
2. Lord Russell of Liverpool, *The Knights of Bushido: A Short History of Japanese War Crimes* (London: Greenhill Books, 2005), 139
3. *Ten Escape from Tojo* by Commander Melvin H. McCoy, USN, and Lieutenant Colonel S.M. Mellnik, USA as told to Lieutenant Welbourn Kelley, USNR, March 1944, Franklin D. Roosevelt Library and Museum, Safe Files, Box 3
4. *Ibid.*
5. *Ibid.*
6. Lord Russell of Liverpool, *The Knights of Bushido: A Short History of Japanese War Crimes* (London: Greenhill Books, 2005), 234
7. *Ten Escape from Tojo* by Commander Melvin H. McCoy, USN, and Lieutenant Colonel S.M. Mellnik, USA as told to Lieutenant Welbourn Kelley, USNR, March 1944, Franklin D. Roosevelt Library and Museum, Safe Files, Box 3
8. *Ibid.*
9. *Ibid.*
10. *Ibid.*
11. *Ibid.*
12. *Ibid.*
13. *Ibid.*
14. *Ibid.*
15. *Ibid.*
16. *Ibid.*
17. *Ibid.*
18. *Ibid.*

19. *Ibid.*
20. *Ibid.*
21. William Dyess, *The Dyess Story: The Eye-Witness Account of the Death March from Bataan and the Narrative of Experiences in Japanese Prison Camps and of Eventual Escape* (New York: G.P. Putnam's Sons, 1944), 149
22. *Ibid*: 159
23. *Ibid*: 166
24. *Ibid*: 166
25. *Ibid*: 175
26. *Ten Escape from Tojo* by Commander Melvin H. McCoy, USN, and Lieutenant Colonel S.M. Mellnik, USA as told to Lieutenant Welbourn Kelley, USNR, March 1944, Franklin D. Roosevelt Library and Museum, Safe Files, Box 3
27. William Dyess, *The Dyess Story: The Eye-Witness Account of the Death March from Bataan and the Narrative of Experiences in Japanese Prison Camps and of Eventual Escape* (New York: G.P. Putnam's Sons, 1944), 176
28. *Ten Escape from Tojo* by Commander Melvin H. McCoy, USN, and Lieutenant Colonel S.M. Mellnik, USA as told to Lieutenant Welbourn Kelley, USNR, March 1944, Franklin D. Roosevelt Library and Museum, Safe Files, Box 3
29. William Dyess, *The Dyess Story: The Eye-Witness Account of the Death March from Bataan and the Narrative of Experiences in Japanese Prison Camps and of Eventual Escape* (New York: G.P. Putnam's Sons, 1944), 178
30. *Ibid*: 181
31. *Ten Escape from Tojo* by Commander Melvin H. McCoy, USN, and Lieutenant Colonel S.M. Mellnik, USA as told to Lieutenant Welbourn Kelley, USNR, March 1944, Franklin D. Roosevelt Library and Museum, Safe Files, Box 3
32. *Ibid.*
33. *Ibid.*

Chapter 6: Three Thousand Miles to Freedom

1. John Boyd, *Tenko! Rangoon Jail* (Paducah, KY: Turner Publishing Company), 1996, 53

2. *The Reconnaissance Corps*, regiments.org/regiments/uk/cav/ recce.htm, accessed 28 May 2012

3. Colin Smith, *Singapore Burning: Heroism and Surrender in World War II* (London: Viking, 2005), 439

4. *Ibid*: 439

5. John Boyd, *Tenko! Rangoon Jail* (Paducah, KY: Turner Publishing Company, 1996), 54

6. *Ibid*: 54

7. *Ibid*: 54

8. *Ibid*: 54

9. *Ibid*: 54

10. Allied deaths were: Britain 6,318; Australia 2,815; Netherlands 2,490; United States c.356, plus a handful of New Zealanders and Canadians

11. John Boyd, *Tenko! Rangoon Jail* (Paducah, KY: Turner Publishing Company, 1996), 56

12. *Ibid*: 56

13. *Ibid*: 57

14. *Ibid*: 58

15. *Ibid*: 58

16. *Ibid*: 59

17. *Ibid*: 60

18. *Ibid*: 62

19. *Ibid*: 62

20. *Ibid*: 62

21. Box 263, Exhibit 1991, Japanese Expeditionary Forces in China, Document No. 626-A: *Regulations For Punishment of Enemy Air Crews*, 13 August 1942, MacMillan Brown Library, University of Canterbury, Christchurch, New Zealand.

22. The Wartime Memories Project – Rangoon Jail POW Camp, wartimememories.co.uk/pow/rangoon.html, accessed 30 May 2009

23. *Ibid*.

24. John Boyd, *Tenko! Rangoon Jail* (Paducah, KY: Turner Publishing Company, 1996), 68

25. *Ibid*: 68

26. *E Group Consolidated Report British POWs Liberated from Rangoon Jail*, AIR 40/1855, The National Archives (Public Record Office), Kew

27. The Wartime Memories Project – Rangoon Jail POW Camp, wartimememories.co.uk/pow/rangoon.html, accessed 30 May 2009

28. Mark Felton, *The Final Betrayal: Mountbatten, MacArthur and the Fate of Japanese POWs* (Barnsley: Pen & Sword Books, 2010), 89

Chapter 7: Officially Dead

1. Gregory Urwin, *Facing Fearful Odds: The Siege of Wake Island* (University of Nebraska Press, 1997), 192

2. John Wukovits, *Pacific Alamo: The Battle for Wake Island* (New American Library, 2004)

3. Bryan Perrett, *Last Stand: Famous Battles Against the Odds* (Weidenfeld Military, 1992)

4. Gregory Urwin, *Facing Fearful Odds: The Siege of Wake Island* (University of Nebraska Press, 1997), 537

5. *The Life of Rear Admiral Winfield Scott Cunningham* by Greg R. Cunningham, chuckhawks.com/admiral_cunningham.htm, accessed 20 March 2012

6. *Ibid.*

7. *Ibid.*

8. *Total Listing of Casualties and Disposition of Wake Island Personnel, 1941–1945*, File 1L (United States Marine Corps Historical Archives)

9. *The Life of Rear Admiral Winfield Scott Cunningham* by Greg R. Cunningham, chuckhawks.com/admiral_cunningham.htm, accessed 20 March 2012

10. *Despatch on Surrender of Hong Kong, Sir Mark Young to Secretary of State for the Colonies, 12 September 1945*, CO968/98/6, The National Archives (TNA): Public Record Office (PRO)

11. Stella Dong, *Shanghai: The Rise and Fall of a Decadent City* (New York: William Morrow, Perennial, 2001), 276-277

12. *Despatch on Surrender of Hong Kong, Sir Mark Young to Secretary of State for the Colonies, 12 September 1945*, CO968/98/6, The National Archives (TNA): Public Record Office (PRO)

13. *The Life of Rear Admiral Winfield Scott Cunningham* by Greg R. Cunningham, chuckhawks.com/admiral_cunningham.htm, accessed 20 March 2012

14. *Ibid.*
15. *Ibid.*
16. *Ibid.*
17. *Ibid.*
18. *Ibid.*
19. *Ibid.*
20. *Ibid.*
21. *Ibid.*
22. *Ibid.*
23. *Ibid.*
24. *Ibid.*

Chapter 8: March into Oblivion

1. Imperial Japanese Army, Box 263, Exhibit 1978, Document No. 1114-B: *Regarding the outline for the disposal of Prisoners of War according to the change of situation, a notification, Army-Asia-Secret No. 2257, by the Vice War Minister*, 11 March 1945, MacMillan Brown Library, University of Canterbury, Christchurch, New Zealand.
2. Lord Russell of Liverpool, *The Knights of Bushido: A Short History of Japanese War Crimes* (London, Greenhill Books, 2002), 143
3. *Laden, Fevered, Starved – The POWs of Sandakan, North Borneo, 1945*, Department of Veterans' Affairs, Australian Government, dva.gov.au, accessed 6 August 2008
4. Lord Russell of Liverpool, *The Knights of Bushido: A Short History of Japanese War Crimes* (London, Greenhill Books, 2002), 143
5. *The Marches, Australia's War 1939–1945*, ww2australia.gov.au, accessed 1 September 2012
6. *Laden, Fevered, Starved – The POWs of Sandakan, North Borneo, 1945*, Department of Veterans' Affairs, Australian Government, dva.gov.au, accessed 6 August 2008
7. *Ibid.*
8. *Ibid.*
9. *Statement by Gunner Campbell, 2/10th Field Regiment, 21 August 1945*, 1010/4/27, AWM 54, Australian War Memorial, Canberra
10. *Ibid.*

Notes

11. *Ibid.*
12. *Laden, Fevered, Starved – The POWs of Sandakan, North Borneo, 1945*, Department of Veterans' Affairs, Australian Government, dva.gov.au, accessed 6 August 2008
13. *Laden, Fevered, Starved – The POWs of Sandakan, North Borneo, 1945*, Department of Veterans' Affairs, Australian Government, dva.gov.au, accessed 3 September 2012
14. *Ibid.*
15. *Ibid.*
16. *Statement by Gunner Campbell, 2/10th Field Regiment, 21 August 1945*, 1010/4/27, AWM 54, Australian War Memorial, Canberra
17. *Ibid.*
18. *Ibid.*
19. *Ibid.*
20. *Ibid.*
21. *Statement made to Major H W S Jackson by Gulunting of Kampong Sapi, at Beluran, North Borneo, 12 January 1947*, papers of Lieutenant Colonel W S Jackson, ?item 9, part 1, PR 84/231, Australian War Memorial, Canberra
22. *Ibid.*
23. *Laden, Fevered, Starved – The POWs of Sandakan, North Borneo, 1945*, Department of Veterans' Affairs, Australian Government, dva.gov.au, accessed 6 August 2008
24. *Ibid.*
25. *Laden, Fevered, Starved – The POWs of Sandakan, North Borneo, 1945*, Department of Veterans' Affairs, Australian Government, dva.gov.au, accessed 3 September 2012
26. *'A lofty hero moved by rescue mission'* by Alan Ramsey, *Sydney Morning Herald*, 9 August 2008
27. *Ibid.*
28. *Laden, Fevered, Starved – The POWs of Sandakan, North Borneo, 1945*, Department of Veterans' Affairs, Australian Government, dva.gov.au, accessed 6 August 2008
29. *Laden, Fevered, Starved – The POWs of Sandakan, North Borneo, 1945*, Department of Veterans' Affairs, Australian Government, dva.gov.au, accessed 3 September 2012
30. *'A lofty hero moved by rescue mission'* by Alan Ramsey, *Sydney Morning Herald*, 9 August 2008

31. *Laden, Fevered, Starved – The POWs of Sandakan, North Borneo, 1945*, Department of Veterans' Affairs, Australian Government, dva.gov.au, accessed 3 September 2012

Appendix B: Roll of Honour

1. This list is not exhaustive

Bibliography

Archives

Australian War Memorial, Canberra

Statement by Gunner Campbell, 2/10th Field Regiment, 21 August 1945, 1010/4/27, AWM 54

Statement made to Major H W S Jackson by Gulunting of Kampong Sapi, at Beluran, North Borneo, 12 January 1947, papers of Lieutenant Colonel W S Jackson, item 9, part 1, PR 84/231

Franklin D. Roosevelt Library & Museum

Ten Escape from Tojo by Commander Melvin H. McCoy, USN, and Lieutenant Colonel S.M. Mellnik, USA as told to Lieutenant Welbourn Kelley, USNR, March 1944, Safe Files, Box 3

MacMillan Brown Library, University of Canterbury, New Zealand

International Military Tribunal for the Far East, Box 256, Exhibit 1654, Prosecution Document No. 5177: *Affidavit of Lt.-Col. Edmund Macarthur Sheppard of 2/10 Field Ambulance*

International Military Tribunal for the Far East, Box 256, Exhibit 1654, Prosecution Document No. 5179: *Affidavit of Lieutenant Stephen Victor Burt Day of the British Army*

Box 263, Exhibit 1991, Japanese Expeditionary Forces in China, Document No. 626-A: *Regulations For Punishment of Enemy Air Crews*, 13 August 1942

Imperial Japanese Army, Box 263, Exhibit 1978, Document No. 1114-B: *Regarding the outline for the disposal of Prisoners of War according to the change of situation, a notification, Army-Asia-Secret No. 2257, by the Vice War Minister*, 11 March 1945

1504, Tokyo War Trials, 253;33, PX 1504, *Charles Heath, Affidavit re War Crimes at Changi Prisoner of War Camp*, 8 January 1946
1549, Tokyo War Trials, 52; 39, PX 1709, *H.D.W. Sitwell – Affidavit on Treatment in POW Camp on Java*, 10 December 1945

National Archives of Australia, Canberra
'Service Record – VX24597 – Matthews, Lionel'

The National Archives: Public Record Office, Kew
E Group Consolidated Report British POWs Liberated from Rangoon Jail, AIR 40/1855
CO968/98/6, *Despatch on Surrender of Hong Kong, Sir Mark Young to Secretary of State for the Colonies*, 12 September 1945
WO373/103, *The London Omnibus List for Gallant and Distinguished Services in the Field*, 14 February 1947

United States Marine Corps Historical Archives
Total Listing of Casualties and Disposition of Wake Island Personnel, 1941–1945, File 1L

Published Sources
Ashcroft, Lord, *George Cross Heroes: Incredible True Stories of Bravery beyond the Battlefield*, London: Headline Review, 2010
Bayly, Christopher & Harper, Tim, *Forgotten Armies: Britain's Asian Empire & the War with Japan*, London: Allen Lane, 2004
Boyd, John, *Tenko! Rangoon Jail*, Paducah, KY: Turner Publishing Company, 1996
Daws, Gavan, *Prisoners of the Japanese: POWs of the Second World War*, London: Pocket Books, 1994
Dong, Stella, *Shanghai: The Rise and Fall of a Decadent City*, New York: William Morrow, Perennial, 2001
Dyess, William, *The Dyess Story: The Eye-Witness Account of the Death March from Bataan and the Narrative of Experiences in Japanese Prison Camps and of Eventual Escape*, New York: G.P. Putnam's Sons, 1944
Felton, Mark, *Slaughter at Sea: The Story of Japan's Naval War Crimes*, Barnsley: Pen & Sword Maritime, 2007

Felton, Mark, *The Devil's Doctors: Japanese Human Experiments on Allied Prisoners of War*, Barnsley: Pen & Sword Military, 2012

Felton, Mark, *The Final Betrayal: Mountbatten, MacArthur and the Fate of Japanese POWs* (Barnsley: Pen & Sword Books, 2010), 89

Foot, M.R.D., *SOE: An Outline History of the Special Operations Executive*, London: Pimlico, 1999

Gillies, Midge, *The Barbed Wire University: The Real Lives of Prisoners of War in the Second World War*, London: Aurum Press Ltd, 2011

Goodwin, Ralph, *Passport to Eternity*, London: Arthur Baker, 1956

Guest, Freddie, *Escape from the Bloodied Sun*, Norwich: Jarrolds, 1956

Hamond, Robert, *Flame of Freedom: Corporal Ras Pagani's Escape from the Railway of Death*, London: Leo Cooper, 1989

Horner, R.M., *Singapore Diary: The Hidden Journal of Captain R.M. Horner*, London: Spellmount Publishers Ltd, 2007

Lindsay, Oliver, *The Battle for Hong Kong 1941–1945: Hostage to Fortune*, London: Spellmount Publishers Ltd, 2005

MacArthur, Brian, *Surviving the Sword: Prisoners of the Japanese 1942-45*, London: Random House, 2005

Percival, Arthur, *The War in Malaya*, London: Eyre & Spottiswoode, 1949

Perrett, Bryan, *Last Stand: Famous Battles Against the Odds*, Weidenfeld Military, 1992

Lord Russell of Liverpool, *The Knights of Bushido: A Short History of Japanese War Crimes*, London: Greenhill Books, 2002

Smith, Colin, *Singapore Burning: Heroism and Surrender in World War II*, London: Viking, 2005

Urwin, Gregory, *Facing Fearful Odds: The Siege of Wake Island*, University of Nebraska Press, 1997

Wright-Nooth, George, *Prisoner of the Turnip Heads*, London: Lee Cooper, 1994

Wukovits, John, *Pacific Alamo: The Battle for Wake Island*, New American Library, 2004

Newspapers
Eastern Courier (Adelaide)
Sydney Morning Herald
The Argus (Brisbane)
Waiapa Church Gazette

Online Sources

Diary of Brigadier Eric Whitlock Goodman, DSO, MC, 19th February – 11th March 1942, Far East Prisoners of War Association (FEPOW), britain-at-war.org.uk

Hong Kong Escape, hongkongescape.org

Far East Heroes, far-eastern-heroes.org.uk

Laden, Fevered, Starved – The POWs of Sandakan, North Borneo, 1945, Department of Veterans' Affairs, Australian Government, dva.gov.au

'The Bridge Over the River Kwai' by Alan Brown, Children of Far East Prisoners of War, cofepow.org.uk

The Life of Rear Admiral Winfield Scott Cunningham by Greg R. Cunningham, chuckhawks.com/admiral_cunningham.htm

The Marches, Australia's War 1939–1945, ww2australia.gov.au

The Reconnaissance Corps, regiments.org/regiments/uk/cav/recce.htm

The Life of Rear Admiral Winfield Scott Cunningham by Greg R. Cunningham, chuckhawks.com/admiral_cunningham.htm

The Wartime Memories Project – Rangoon Jail POW Camp, wartimememories.co.uk/pow/rangoon.html

Index

MacAthur, Gen. Douglas, 77–8, 80–1
MacDougall, David, 31–3, 36–7, 40
Macmillan, Capt. Peter, 31
Maltby, Maj.-Gen. Christopher, 17–18, 22, 24, 28, 30–1, 43, 46, 58–9
Maltby, Air Vice Marshal Paul, 13–14
Marshall, Sgt. Paul, 94–104
Matthews, Capt. Lionel, 67–8, 71–6, 146
McCoy, Lt.-Cdr. Melvin, 81, 83–6, 89–91, 93–104
McEwan, Maj. Colin, 29, 40, 49
Mellnik, Maj. Stephen, 82–4, 86–9, 91, 93–104
MI9, 3
Ming, Joe, 74
Mission '204', 40
Montague, Cdr. Hugh, 31–5
Moody, SSgt. Samuel, 80
Moruzumi, Sgt. Maj. Hisao, 159–64
Moth, HMS, 24–5
Moxham, L-Bdr. William, 150–64

Nagatomo, Lt.-Col. Y., 114
Newbigging, Brig. Terence, 11
Newnham, Col. Lanceray, 43, 51, 57–8, 60–3
Nimori, Army Interpreter Genichiro, 54
Nitta Maru, 132–3
North British Armed Constabulary (Borneo), 72, 74

Owen-Hughes, Lt.-Col. Harry, 39–40
Outram Road Jail (Singapore), 76
Oxford, Sqn. Ldr. Maxwell, 30–1

Pagani, Cpl. Roy, 105–27
Parker, Maj.-Gen. George, 78
Parson, Lt. Tommy, 37
Pears, Lt.-Cdr. A.L., 26
Pearson, Brig. S.H., 112
Percival, Lt.-Gen. Arthur, 10, 19, 67–8
Perth, HMAS, 111
Peterel, HMS, 22–4, 136–7
Po, Thin, 117–18
Pocomoke, USS, 160–1
Polkinghorn, Lt. Stephen, 23–4, 136–7
Prince of Wales, HMS, 112
Pye, Vice-Adm. William, 129

Quezon, President Manuel, 80–1, 104
Quittenton, WO2 Matthew, 20

Reither, Pvt. Herman, 162
Ride, Lt.-Col. Lindsay, 46–7, 56, 59–60
Robertson, Superintendent William, 30–1, 34
Robin, HMS, 28, 32
Roosevelt, President Franklin D., 78, 86, 104
Ross, Ted, 31–3
Royal Navy:
    2nd Motor Torpedo Boat Flotilla, 26–30, 33–4

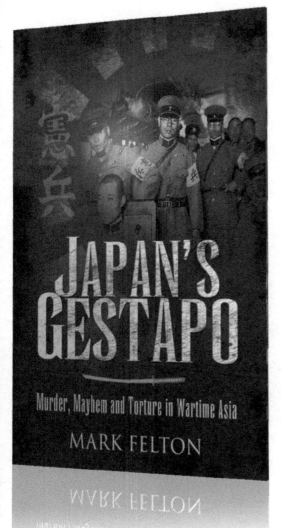

JAPAN'S GESTAPO

Murder, Mayhem and Torture in Wartime Asia

MARK FELTON

9781848846807 •
PB • 8 B&W plates •
224 pages • £12.99

This disturbing book reveals the extent of the truly shocking activities of the Kempeitai, Japan's feared military and secret police. The book opens by explaining the origins, organization and roles of the Kempeitai apparatus, which exercised virtually unlimited power throughout the Japanese Empire. The author reveals their criminal and collaborationist networks, which extorted huge sums of money from hapless citizens and businesses. They ran the Allied POW gulag system which treated captives with merciless and murderous brutality. Other Kempeitai activities included biological and chemical experiments on live subjects, the Maruta vivisection campaign and widespread slave labour, including 'Comfort Women' drawn from all races.

The author backs up his text with first hand testimonies from those survivors who suffered at the hands of this evil organization. He examines how the guilty were brought to justice and the resulting claims for compensation. As a result *Japan's Gestapo* provides comprehensive evidence of the ruthlessness of the Kempeitai against the white and Asian peoples under their control.

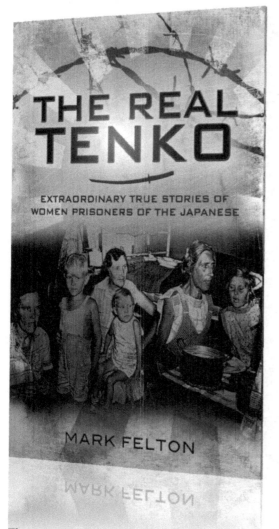

THE REAL TENKO

EXTRAORDINARY TRUE STORIES OF
WOMEN PRISONERS OF THE JAPANESE

MARK FELTON

9781848845503 •
PB • 8 B&W plates •
176 pages • £12.99

The mistreatment and captivity of women by the Japanese is a little known and poorly documented aspect of the Second World War. In *The Real Tenko*, Mark Felton redresses this omission with a typically well researched yet necessarily gruesome account of the plight of Allied service-women, female civilians and local women in Japanese hands.

Among the atrocities shamefully committed by the Emperor's forces were numerous massacres of nurses; that at Alexandra Hospital, Singapore being perhaps the best known. The lack of respect for their defeated enemies extended in full measure to both European and Asian women and their vulnerability was all too often shockingly exploited. Those who found themselves imprisoned fared little better and suffered appalling indignities and starvation.

The Real Tenko is a disturbing and shocking testimony both to the callous and cruel behaviour of the Japanese and to the courage and fortitude of those who suffered at their hands.

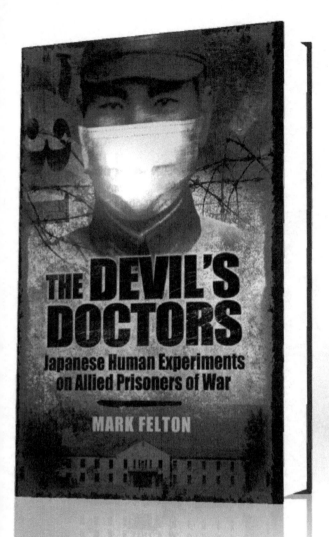

THE DEVIL'S DOCTORS
Japanese Human Experiments on Allied Prisoners of War

MARK FELTON

9781848844797 •
HB • 8 B&W plates •
208 pages • £19.99

The brutal Japanese treatment of Allied POWs in the Second World War has been well documented in numerous moving accounts. However *The Devil's Doctors* is the first study revealing the Japanese medical experiments on Allied POWs.

The experiences of British, Australian and American POWs, whether on the Burma Railway, in the mines of Formosa and in camps across the Far East, were bad enough. But the mistreatment of those used as guinea pigs in medical experiments was in a different league. The author reveals distressing evidence of Unit 731 experiments involving US, British and Australian prisoners in Northern China, notably Mukden POW Camp, Hainan Island, New Guinea and in Japan. These resulted in loss of life and extreme suffering.

WHAT THE CRITICS SAID:

'Uncovers the shocking links between Allied POWs and the infamous Unit 731, at the Mukden POW Camp in Northern China, and proves that the British and American governments co-operated post-war, using data derived from Japanese experiments for chemical and biological warfare purposes.'
THE GUARDIAN

9781848842861 •
HB • 8 B&W plates •
208 pages • £19.99

In *The Last Nazis*, Mark Felton has written a fascinating investigative book tracing the hunt for surviving Nazi war criminals and, in so doing, brings the story of the sixty-five year hunt for Nazi war criminals up to date. He reveals that there are a surprising number of war criminals remaining alive and free today despite the on-going campaign by the Simon Weisenthal Center, which launched 'Operation Last Chance' in 2008. It is not generally known that, since 2001, no less than seventy-six legal decisions have been won against perpetrators and their collaborators, half of them in the USA.

The author vividly demonstrates that the crimes perpetrated by the Nazis are no less appalling for the passage of time. He also covers those which died recently before trial, as well as those who have succeeded in escaping justice or only suffered very minor punishment.

WHAT THE CRITICS SAID:

'This 200-page hardback is designed to shock readers with accounts of the heinous crimes commited by evil men and women. It succeeds.'
DOVER EXPRESS, FOLKSTONE HERALD, DEAL EXPRESS

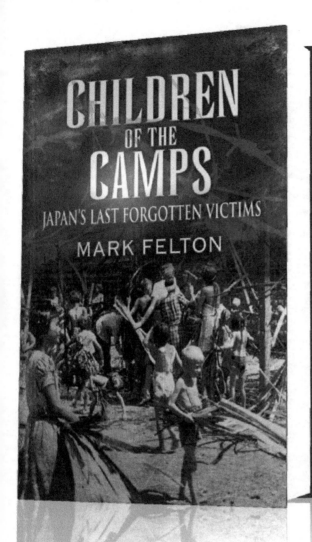

9781848842618 •
HB • 8 B&W plates •
208 pages • £19.99

Children of the Camps tells the heart-rending stories of Caucasian and Eurasian children who were imprisoned within Japanese internment camps throughout Asia during the Second World War.

The Japanese treatment of Allied children was as harsh and murderous as that of their parents' and military POWs, but this shameful episode has been largely overlooked. The author has gathered together numerous survivors' moving and disturbing testimonies. We learn how children of all ages were plucked from comfortable colonial lives to endure terrible camp conditions. Many were separated from their parents or saw their families destroyed by the Japanese. Survival became a daily game with their lives constantly threatened by disease, starvation and physical abuse. Most regularly witnessed episodes of bestial violence that no child should ever see, and the entire cumulative experience inevitably had a deep and lasting effect on their subsequent adult lives. They are among the last victims of Japanese aggression and, even after sixty years later, many carry the mental and physical scars of that atrocious episode.

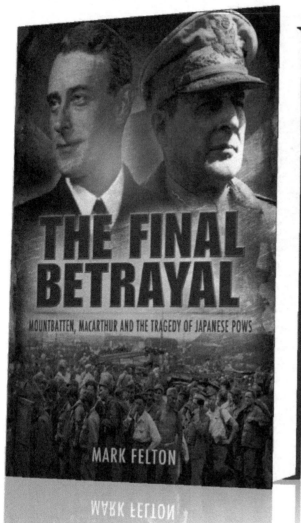

9781848840942 •
HB • 8 B&W plates •
192 pages • £19.99

The Final Betrayal provides sensational new evidence about the little known but shameful delay in rescuing allied POWs between the unconditional surrender of Japan on 14 August 1945 and the arrival of Allied liberation forces in Japanese occupied territories after 2 September 1945. The Japanese used this golden opportunity to destroy vast amounts of documentation concerning war crimes and to set their house in order before Allied war crimes investigators arrived. POW facilities and medical experimentation installations were either abandoned or destroyed. During this period groups of Allied POWs were brutally murdered and countless more died needlessly from starvation, disease and ill-treatment.

The Author reveals that the blame rests principally with General MacArthur, Supreme Allied Commander in the Pacific. Incredibly MacArthur expressly forbade any Allied forces from liberating Japanese occupied territories before he had taken the formal Japanese surrender aboard the USS *Missouri* in Tokyo Bay on 2 September 1945. Vice Admiral Lord Mountbatten, Commanding Allied Forces in South-east Asia, protested against this perverse policy, convinced that MacArthur's vanity would condemn many starving and sick British and Commonwealth POWs to death; the majority of American POWs were already being liberated in the Philippines and elsewhere.